From Market to Stock Market

The Story of Dunelm

From Market to Stock Market

The Story of Dunelm

Bill Adderley
with Ivan Fallon

UNICORN

To my six grandchildren
Never forget where you came from

Published in 2025 by
Unicorn, an imprint of Unicorn Publishing Group
Charleston Studio
Meadow Business Centre
Lewes BN8 5RW
www.unicornpublishing.org

Text copyright © 2025 Bill Adderley

All rights reserved. No part of the contents of this book may be reproduced, stored in or introduced into a retrieval system, or transmitted, in any form or by any means (electronic, mechanical, photocopying, recording or otherwise), without the prior written permission of the copyright holder and the above publisher of this book.

Every effort has been made to trace copyright holders and to obtain their permission for the use of copyrighted material. The publisher apologises for any errors or omissions and would be grateful to be notified of any corrections that should be incorporated in future reprints or editions of this book.

ISBN 978 1 917458 12 2
10 9 8 7 6 5 4 3 2 1

Design by newtonworks.uk
Printed and bound in Great Britain by Bell and Bain Ltd, Glasgow

Contents

	Preface	1
Chapter 1	**Donegal**	11
Chapter 2	**My Father**	21
Chapter 3	**School Days**	40
Chapter 4	**Woolworths – the Great Days**	44
Chapter 5	**Manager**	59
Chapter 6	**Jean**	65
Chapter 7	**End of an Era**	74
Chapter 8	**Leicester Market**	84
Chapter 9	**Simply Value for Money**	89
Chapter 10	**Some Hard Lessons**	96
Chapter 11	**Dunelm is Born**	107
Chapter 12	**Saturday Sales**	110

Chapter 13	**Churchgate**	119
Chapter 14	**Golf**	132
Chapter 15	**The Dunelm Model**	139
Chapter 16	**Takeover Bid**	146
Chapter 17	**Taking a Step Back**	151
Chapter 18	**East Street**	154
Chapter 19	**The Sweater Shop**	158
Chapter 20	**Houses**	162
Chapter 21	**Stock Market**	165
Chapter 22	**Raid on M&S**	181
	Postscript	189
Appendix	**Stamford School Lecture**	198
	Acknowledgements	204
	Index	205

Preface

It was November 1978, the beginning of the Winter of Discontent that brought Margaret Thatcher to power in Britain, and I was out of a job. For fifteen years I had worked for Woolworths, starting as a fifteen-year-old 'Saturday boy' sweeping the floors and moving up the ladder until I reached the giddy heights of manager of the West Bromsgrove store in Birmingham. I had been a loyal employee, seen as a bit of a high-flier and might have gone to the very top if I'd stayed on.

But the company had changed over my time there and, following a heated disagreement with a hostile manager from head office, I resigned. For the first time in my life, I found myself unemployed. It was a strange feeling.

After a week of feeling sorry for myself, I set out to find another job. I thought I had a good reputation in the retail industry, and I was prepared to accept almost anything just to get back on my feet again.

Early December proved to be a bad time to begin looking for a job, however, and I found my old contacts polite but evasive. 'It's coming up to Christmas, Bill, and we're not taking anyone on just now. Come back in January or February and we might have something for you,' said an old Woolworths colleague, now a store manager at Morrisons. When I got a similar response from others, including Marks & Spencer and Tesco, I suddenly twigged: Woolworths had spread the word that I was a bit of a troublemaker. Nobody wanted me.

I had bills to pay and I was running out of money with which to pay them. Because I'd resigned from Woolworths I got only a nominal compensation. (I later challenged this in court but lost.) I had recently bought a house in Coalville, near Leicester, my last store before West Brom, extending myself to the limit, and my wife Jean and I seriously discussed putting it on the market. Interest rates were sky-high at the time – 8 per cent – and my monthly mortgage payments came to £800 a month. After my December payment, I would have only £800 left in the bank.

After being fobbed off by the big shopping groups, I gave up and looked for something else. More in desperation than in hope, I had a thought. In my last days at Woolworths people were clamouring for home deliveries, but Woolworths was a high street chain and didn't deliver, so customers had to make their own arrangements. There was a business opportunity there, and I was desperate enough to try it. I laid out £200 of my precious cash on an old Bedford bread van with a central door at the back and the brand 'Wonderloaf' emblazoned on the side, and on a freezing mid-winter's morning, I got up early, scraped the ice off the windscreen and drove to one of the semi-industrial estates that surrounded Leicester. Something was always being collected or delivered there and my intention was to knock on doors, asking for business.

I was just deciding where to start when a yellow Rolls-Royce, followed by a Porsche driven by a smart-looking lady, swept past me and drove into a warehouse a hundred yards further on. I couldn't resist following them and found myself in the most sumptuous office I had ever seen. (I learned later it had been furnished by Harrods.)

The man in the Rolls-Royce greeted me courteously and asked me what he could do for me. I introduced myself, told him I was a former Woolworths manager looking for work and I could do any deliveries he wanted. In turn he introduced himself as Keith Childs and the lady in the Porsche as his wife. We chatted for a few minutes about the state of the economy and the terrible winter the country was experiencing until, finally, I asked him, 'What do you do here?' Whatever it was, I thought it must be very profitable to support him in such style.

'I import shoes and supply the big department stores and shoe shops,' he said, readily enough.

'Well, have you got any seconds that I could sell on the market?' I responded without even giving it proper thought. We sometimes offered seconds or discontinued lines in

Woolworths as a special offer but I had never sold anything on the market in my life. At that moment it suddenly seemed like a good idea.

He took me into a room at the back and waved his hand at stacks of boxes piled up to the ceiling. 'That's a big order of slippers that's just come in from Korea,' he said, 'and they're faulty. I was just going to put them all in a landfill.' He opened a box, got out a pair and showed them to me. They were still in their original cellophane, all labelled Freeman, Hardy and Willis, a big high street shoe shop chain, and labelled £3.99. We sold something similar in Woolworth for about the same price and, after a quick examination, I couldn't see much wrong with these.

'I'll take them off your hands,' I found myself saying before I could think about it. 'How much do you want for them?' He considered that for a moment.

'There's 20,000 pairs there. You can have as many as you want at 50p each. But you'll have to remove that label before you sell them.'

I took a deep gulp, thought of my dwindling bank balance, and said, 'Well, I'll have five hundred quids' worth. That's a thousand pairs.'

We did the deal, I paid him in cash, loaded the slippers into the van and went straight home and stacked them up in the house. Jean was out shopping and when she came home she gazed in bemusement at these boxes piled up in the kitchen and hallway. 'I spent all the money. I've bought these slippers,' I confessed.

'What are you going to do with them?' asked Jean, still reeling from the shock.

'I'm going to sell them on the market,' I said with a lot more confidence than I felt. We had often shopped in the market in Leicester, as everyone did in those days, and I had a hazy idea of taking a stall there. 'But we've got to remove the price first.'

That's when Jean really came into her own. Most wives would have blown a fuse, and I was expecting a real bollocking, but she was remarkably calm. 'Right. Well, let's get stuck in.'

After putting our two young boys to bed, we started work that evening. Using the kitchen table as a workbench, I carefully slit open each box, took the slippers out of their wrappers, removed the sticky label with the point of a long carving fork and passed the box across to Jean. She then used nail varnish remover to erase the £3.99 price tag and neatly repacked the slippers into their boxes. We'd done about half of them when I began to flag. 'Shall we pack up for the night and go to bed?'

Jean said 'No', and we worked on. Only later did we realise that we were both high on the fumes of the nail varnish remover, which we'd been sniffing all night.

I made some rough signs with '99p a pair' written on them and early the next morning I went down to the Leicester market with a van load of slippers. The market, the biggest in

Britain, had nearly 300 stalls, but most of them were occupied by regular traders and were not for rent. However, someone told me there were usually stalls available during the week that were allotted on a first-come, first-served basis (you could never get anything on Saturdays, the busiest day).

The market didn't open until 9 am, but I wanted to be first in the queue to get a stall and arrived at 7.45 am. I waited outside the office until at nine a little glass window slid across and a face appeared. I registered my name and address, and the guy told me I'd have to wait until the regulars were dealt with before he served 'the casuals'. I found a seat and watched as traders, not all regulars, joined the queue, thinking confidently, 'I was first. This is it, I've cracked it.' Then an extraordinary-looking guy sauntered in wearing a sheepskin coat, bottleneck glasses and hair plastered down as if it had been dipped in a frying pan. Some of the others seemed to know him and addressed his as 'Swag' and when I asked someone near me who he was, he said, 'He's Nev Bray – but we all call him Swag. He's quite a character. We often see him here when he's got something to sell.'

As time passed and my name had not been called, I began to panic. Other people were getting their tickets and setting off for their allotted stalls and the queue had come to an end when the guy called out, 'Bray, D12', and Swag, who was last in the queue, went over and came away with a ticket. Then the hatch slammed closed and I was left stuck there.

PREFACE

I knocked on the glass window and told the guy, 'That's not fair. I was first and I need the money more than these people.' But he just grunted.

'There's nothing today, mate.' He slammed the window shut again. Disconsolately, I wandered through the market wondering how everyone got preference over me. I spotted Swag laying out his stall and went over to him.

'Excuse me,' I said politely. 'Can I ask you something? I'm just curious. I was first in the queue this morning for a stall, well before anyone else. How come you've got your stall and I didn't get one and you were last in?' He was a bit of a rough-looking bloke but because I had approached him in the right way, he turned out to be very helpful.

'You've got to sort out the Toby,' he said.

'What's the Toby?' I asked, puzzled.

'Have you never heard of a Toby? Toby jug,' he explained. 'Always with a bent handle twisted up behind his back. The superintendent, the guy behind the glass – we call him Toby. He's the one you gotta settle with. For an extra fiver, he'll give you a stall all right.'

So I went back and banged on the window until Toby's head appeared, demanding, 'Yeah?'

'Look, I was first in the queue this morning and I didn't get a stall. But I'm coming back tomorrow and if I get a stall, I'll be very, very grateful.' He just grunted again and closed the window.

I went home, deeply depressed, and that night I sat in the bath and I started crying and I couldn't stop crying. I thought I'd lost everything: I couldn't get a job, I had no money, I had gambled everything we had on a deal that hadn't come off and I couldn't meet the next mortgage payment.

But the next morning I decided to give it another go, and once again I was first in the queue when the guy pulled back the shutter. This time it was different. The rental for a stall was £4 a day but I gave him a £10 note and told him to keep the change. I got my stall.

Within minutes of opening for business, I sold my first pair of slippers, and went on selling them all day. The next day was the same and the day after that was even busier. Everyone loved the slippers, which were a genuine bargain at 99p, and a week before Christmas I sold out and went back to Mr Childs for more. In a three-week period I made £8,000 profit, all in cash of course, no cheques, and every night when I got home, I put the day's takings into a little box under the bed.

Over Christmas, Jean and I talked a lot about what I should do next. I had been incredibly lucky with the slippers, but how was I going to follow it up? How could I turn this into a sustainable business? After less than a month on the market, I'd earned more than I was paid in an entire year at Woolworths and nobody had bothered me – I was my own boss. That evening, as we were counting the cash, I said to Jean: 'You know, there's something in this. I've been a bum for a month

PREFACE

and I'm better off than I was after fifteen years working for Woolworths. I think I'll stick to being a bum!'

And that's how it began. Over the next twenty years, the little business which started life on that stall in Leicester market in December 1979 would grow into one of the most successful retail chains in Britain.

I called it Dunelm.

Chapter 1

Donegal

Whenever someone asks me where my roots are, I always say, 'Donegal', in Ireland. Specifically, Clonmany, on the north-western corner of the island of Ireland, between the mouths of Lough Swilly on the west, and Lough Foyle, which marks the border with Northern Ireland, on the east.

Most of the happiest memories of my childhood are there. My mother, Bridget Gill, was born in Clonmany, the daughter of a farmer whose family had tilled the land for at least four generations and probably more. I visited Clonmany every year as a boy and even now, more than sixty years later, when I need space and time to think, I sometimes climb into my car and drive there just to see the sea and taste the air.

For a boy growing up in a family of six on a council estate in Yorkshire in the 1950s, Clonmany was paradise. My memory now is of endless, golden days when we went to the seaside, fished in the rivers, or helped my grandfather in the fields. In mid-summer, there was light over the Atlantic until nearly midnight and it was bright again a few hours later. I don't recall the days when it rained, but I suppose it must have done.

What I remember most clearly is the excitement with which we packed our bags and set off from Leeds on the long journey by train, boat and bus to the remotest county in Ireland. That was the most wonderful feeling in the world – no school for two whole months, just endless summer days stretching ahead seemingly forever.

My grandparents, Willie and Kate Gill, were always there to greet us with a turf fire going and the kettle permanently on the boil. They lived in a simple thatched cottage with no running water, no inside bathroom and no electricity. Every drop of water had to be carried into the house in buckets from the mountain stream just below the house; the lavatory was a hole in the ground with a seat over it in a tiny shed with a tin roof (I have a picture of myself in short trousers walking back from it to the cottage); and light inside the cottage was provided by a Tilley lamp or candles. The family had their own bit of bog where they cut their turf, which, once it had dried, burned for days. My grandfather kept the outside of the cottage immaculate, whitewashing the walls every year and fixing the roof before the winter gales, and inside my grandmother made sure it was always neat as a pin.

My mother was born in that cottage on 15 August 1923, the eldest of six children. Her father farmed about ten acres of poor, hill-side land, where he kept cows, a large horse that pulled the plough (and did everything else), and harvested his meagre crops. My mother used to describe how the family basically lived off the farm. Dinner, eaten at midday, seldom varied: 'poundies', the local name for mashed potatoes mixed with scallions (spring onions), butter and milk, sometimes with a bit of meat, but never on Fridays – the Catholic Church proclaimed it was a sin to eat meat on a Friday, so occasionally they had fish. That's what we lived on too on our summer visits. Nothing much had changed.

My grandparents always reminded me of John Wayne and Maureen O'Hara in *The Quiet Man*, the film that was made down the coast in County Mayo. They wore the same clothes, the men in collarless shirts and waistcoats even as they ploughed the fields and the women always in shapeless black dresses. I have a picture of my grandparents in their old age looking just like that, my grandfather chewing on his briar pipe. He once showed me how he put the perforated top of an old pepper pot over the bowl, which could keep it going all day, winter and summer.

Although they mostly spoke English in my time, my grandparents grew up in families where the first language was Irish and, according to the 1911 Census, my grandmother could read and write in both Irish and English and my grandfather could read English but not write. Both sides of the family are listed as farmers going back as many generations as far as the records go.

My grandfather was born in Clonmany into what must have been extreme poverty. The potato famine of the 1840s, when more than a million Irish people died and another million emigrated, had devastated the rural areas of Donegal, leaving the survivors – those who hadn't left for America – on the edge of starvation. Medical treatment was beyond their reach: the story I always heard was that my grandfather's father, my great-grandfather, bled to death after having a tooth extracted in Clonmany, leaving his large family to scrape a living somehow off their little farm.

Many families in Donegal survived from the remittances sent back from a brother or cousin who had emigrated to America or, more likely, England where for the next hundred years they specialised in digging the tunnels for the London tube trains. My mother had grand-uncles, uncles and cousins who did exactly that and, even today, in prosperous Ireland, the tradition lives on. I often meet locals in the pubs in Donegal who have just returned from London, flush with cash, from working on 'the tunnels'.

My great-grandmother Margaret was born in 1865 and the 1911 Census, by which stage she was a widow, lists her as 'farmer' and my great-grandfather's occupation as 'farmer's son' (he was only fourteen at the time of the census). All of them are listed as 'literate'.

When people talk about poverty now, I don't think they have any notion of how poor the people in rural Ireland were, particularly in Donegal. I remember my grannie telling me that, as a little girl in Clonmany, word came through that a car was about to pass through the town. They had never seen a car before, so she and her sisters ran down to the road where she suddenly realised that all their feet were bleeding – none of them had shoes.

Many years later, RTE, the Irish radio and TV station, interviewed my grandparents on the occasion of their sixty-sixth wedding anniversary. They were the longest married couple in Ireland. The interviewer asked my grannie: 'What was it you saw in Willie when you first met him?'

My grannie thought about that for a moment and then replied, perfectly seriously, 'He had his own donkey!'

The interview went out on national radio and in the following week about thirty engaged couples came to ask them for advice.

Their tough way of life and diet did them no harm: they both lived to be ninety-nine, dying within a few months of each other.

My mother, like most of the local children, left school at twelve to help her mother. She went to England, as I shall describe, when she was still in her teens. All her life she loved to go back to Clonmany and we loved to go with her. Every summer, she rented a cottage down the road from my grandparents and over the years I got to know every inch of the Gill family farm and can see every rocky outcrop and every small field in my mind's eye. There were no fences – just dry-stone walls, built by skilled artisans when the fields were cleared in the eighteenth century. In the summer the cattle grazed on the hillside above the farm where the calves were fattened up to be taken to the market before winter. I have a clear memory of the cows being brought down by the collie dog to be milked in the evening by my grandfather.

There was a meadow that my grandfather originally cut with a sickle, later graduating to a scythe – but never a tractor. The grass lay on the ground for a few days, hopefully in the sun, and we helped him build it into simple haycocks, trampling it down as my grandfather and uncles expertly threw it up on their pitchforks. It would later be brought into the barn to feed the cows through the winter.

One of my little chores was to fetch the water from the stream for my grannie, who poured it into the large enamel bowl in the corner of the kitchen that was always kept filled. It was used for everything, including making tea, which my grandfather, like most people of his generation, drank strong and sweet, stirring four or five teaspoons of sugar into a mug.

There was no bath or shower, yet somehow my grandfather, even if he'd worked in the fields all day in his shirt and waistcoat, always appeared neat and tidy. My grandmother never had a hair out of place.

The farm was near the Atlantic Coast and there were wonderful beaches – we called them 'strands' – within easy walking distance, long stretches of unspoiled white sand warmed by the Gulf Stream. The sea was still cold, but you soon warmed up if you splashed around vigorously enough, as we always did. None of us were strong swimmers and you had to be careful as there were rip tides that could drag you out to sea in no time. We played endless games on the sand and the dunes behind.

In the evenings or early mornings, we often went fishing in the river – more a stream – near the house. It was nothing elaborate, just worms on a hook that we dangled in the pools and with which we caught brown trout, which were plentiful. They were not big, less than a quarter of a pound, but my grandmother and mother were always delighted to get them and we often had fresh fish for dinner or for tea, which we ate at six o'clock.

Once I caught a salmon, an accident that took me as much by surprise as it did the salmon. I was fishing for trout when suddenly I saw a great flash of silver and my little rod bent like a bow. It took me a long time to land it and it created great excitement back home – no one had caught a salmon in a long time. Once, they had been plentiful in Ireland's rivers, but by my childhood they were already becoming rare. I'm told they're almost non-existent now.

In late summer there were mushrooms, which we picked in the fields and my grandmother cooked them in a hot pan over the open fire, serving them with salt and butter. We learned to differentiate between the edible mushrooms, which were round and white, from what the older people called 'fairy' mushrooms, much more exotic than the others but deadly poisonous.

My grandparents, like all their neighbours, were devout Catholics and every evening after tea they said the rosary, which, to their disappointment, we never did back home in Leeds, so we were excused. On Sundays everyone would dress in their finest clothes – which meant my grandad put a clean collar and stud on the shirt that he would wear all week – and we all went to mass in St Mary's Church on the main street in Clonmany. The Irish Catholic Church, which ruled supreme in the town and countryside, made missing mass a mortal sin, so no one did – except the Protestants of course, but they had their own, older and grander, church that we never set foot in.

The local parish priest was treated by everyone, including my grandparents, as if he was truly God's messenger on Earth and his every word was taken as gospel. But my mother had an aversion to priests, which I only understood many years later when she was on her deathbed. When I offered to get her a priest she shrank back on the pillow, pleading, 'No, no, I don't want a priest! The priest did something terrible to me when I was a little girl.' I can only guess what it was. We know today how widespread child abuse by the clergy was in those days, but I don't think my grandparents would have believed my mother if she'd told them. Clearly, she never did and kept it a secret until she was dying.

The power of the Catholic Church has long diminished in Ireland, but St Mary's is still full on Sundays and my wife Jean, although she's not a Catholic, likes to go to mass when we're there. But church is not for me.

My grandparents are long gone but the cottage is still there. My Uncle Bill, who looked after them in their final years, stayed on after they died and kept it in good order, but he passed on some years ago and no one lives there now. Grass grows on the thatched roof and the windows and doors have rotted away, leaving the old house open to the Atlantic storms. However, the walls still stand, in bad need of their annual coat of whitewash, but otherwise intact. I visit it every year and I still imagine my lovely grandparents waiting at the door for me. The Ireland of today is a very different country to the one they grew up in and into which my mother was born a hundred years ago. Well into my childhood, Ireland was one of the poorest countries in Europe. Today, Ireland is one of the richest and Donegal is thriving. The Clonmany Festival in the first week of August attracts more than 100,000 people who come from all over the world to enjoy the Gaelic music, dancing and singing. Young people are moving back with their families and along the coast expensive modern bungalows have replaced many of the old cottages. To my eye, they are ugly and should never have been permitted – but that's modern Ireland and many of the old traditions have long gone.

Yet the country I knew as a boy is still remarkably unspoiled, the strands are pristine and the people friendlier than in any other place I have ever lived.

I still have nineteen cousins living near Clonmany and they were very proud when, in 2017, Donegal claimed the top spot on *National Geographic Traveller*'s 'Cool List' of destinations, beating, as the magazine proclaimed, the world's 'culture capitals, hipster hotspots, wild escapes, and places generally keeping it cool'.

I wonder what my grandparents would have made of that?

Chapter 2

My Father

My mother was a country girl, a farmer's daughter brought up in the most rural corner of Ireland. My father, John Joseph Adderley, was a city lad, born in the centre of Dublin on 27 June 1921, six months before Ireland got its independence, so technically he was British. On his birth certificate, his parents, John Joseph and Sarah Adderley (née Fay), gave their address as 8 Upper Oriel Street, a tough area in the Dublin docks on the banks of the River Liffey. My paternal grandfather's occupation is listed simply as 'porter' and his father as 'shoemaker' and various other members of the family are registered as 'labourer'. They are listed as Catholics although Adderley is not an Irish Catholic name and there are very few of them in Ireland today.

My grandfather died when my father was three, so Dad was brought up as a semi-orphan in what was basically a Dublin slum. There were two other boys in the family, Peter and Tom, and an older sister, my Auntie Sarah, born in 1916, and I don't suppose there was much food to go round. Later in life, when

I was very little, my grandmother came over to Leeds to live with us in our little council house and I was told by my father that she 'got into the drink' and he couldn't stop her going to the pub. On the way home one day, she fell off the kerb and banged her head and an ambulance had to be called. She was in bed for months, until finally my mother had had enough and she was sent to live with my Uncle Tom in Birmingham. She died shortly afterwards, probably of the drink.

My father was eighteen, still living at home in Dublin, when the Second World War broke out in September 1939. Ireland remained neutral but, in anticipation of an invasion either by the Germans or – more likely – by the British, the Irish government mobilised its tiny army and recruited another 50,000 troops to defend its borders. My father was one of them.

He was a mild-mannered, gentle man, not cut out to be a soldier, but he wasn't given a choice. After some basic training on the Curragh, in County Kildare, he was posted to Lenan Head Fort, an old British battery guarding the entrance to Lough Swilly in Donegal, which the Irish army had recently taken over after Irish Independence in 1921. It was kept manned, but I doubt its old guns, even though they pointed out to sea, would have been much of a match for a modern battleship, British or German, sailing into the loch with hostile intentions.

I've been there and it's a desolate place, particularly in winter when it gets dark by mid-afternoon, and he and his fellow soldiers must have been very bored. The nearest town – and pub – was Clonmany, just six miles away, near where my eighteen-year-old mother lived on her father's farm. It was a mere stroll for a fit, young soldier.

I'm not sure when or how my parents met but the story with which I grew up was that, soon after the outbreak of war, my mother got a job over the Border in Derry working on the telephones for the British Post Office. My father had something to do with signals for the Irish army and sometimes had to place calls to the British over the Border. Manning the switchboard on the Northern Ireland side was my mother and they got talking, fixed up a date in Clonmany and began going out together.

Within a year my father had deserted from the Irish army, walked across the Border, picked my mother up in Derry and taken her to Belfast where the British army had set up a special recruiting station. No questions were asked: in the early 1940s, the British needed all the young, active recruits they could get, and my father signed up for the duration. He was one of 4,500 Irish soldiers who deserted and crossed the Border illegally to join the British army in the war years. Some of them did it because they were young men in search of adventure, but many others deserted for economic reasons: pay in the Irish army was very low and British soldiers were deemed to be better off (though not by much). In the Second World War, an estimated 80,000 young Irishmen enlisted in the British armed forces (more than 5,000 of them were killed) and more than half a millions, desperate for jobs, went to England to work, replacing the British labourers who were called up. Most of them, including my parents, never went back to live in Ireland.

My father was ordered to report to Catterick Camp in Yorkshire, one of the biggest army bases and training camps in Britain, and he set off by boat and train with my nineteen-year-old mother in tow. The last stop before Catterick was Leeds and, as she could accompany my father no further, my mother had to get off the train – a young girl, on her own for the first time in her life, in a foreign city with no money and nowhere to live. Somehow she found lodgings in Armley Road, a slum area of Leeds, and must have got some sort of job to keep her going, or someone to take her in.

Dad spent the rest of the war as a private in Catterick Camp, visiting my mother when he could, but he wouldn't have had much leave – or money. My sister Kathleen was born in Leeds in 1942 and, unable to cope with a newborn baby on her own, my mother took her back to Donegal when she was only three months old. Little Kathleen was simply absorbed into the large Irish family and my Auntie Anne, my mother's younger sister, more or less adopted her.

One of the war-time stories my father used to relate was the arrival in Leeds of my mother's cousin Niall, who got a job there, probably on a building site. He had clearly picked up the old Clonmany tradition of distilling potcheen (the main ingredient is potatoes) and somehow managed to produce it in a cellar. My father sometimes came home at weekends and, to make a few extra bob, sold it to the neighbours. Inevitably he got caught, was charged with dealing in illegal liquor, and spent three nights in jail. In later years, he made a joke of it, but it can't have been much fun at the time and can't have done much for his army career – he never made it beyond private.

He was eventually demobbed when the Second World War ended in 1945 and he and my mother took up married life together for the first time. They were lucky enough to be given a council house in Middleton, a tough area in South Leeds, and as soon as they could they went back to Donegal to collect their three-year-old daughter Kathleen. Little Kathleen had never known any mother other than Anne and she screamed and screamed when she was taken away, poor thing. I sometimes think that Kathleen's life would have worked out better if my mother had left her there.

Technically, my father was a deserter under Irish law, an offence that in many war-time countries could have had him shot. But in post-war Ireland there were so many returning deserters that it was impractical to court-martial them all, and the Irish government, after a token attempt, gave up. There was no amnesty in Ireland and President Éamon de Valera's vindictive punishment was to cancel their entitlements to gratuities, allowances and pensions and bar them from government-funded employment for a period of seven years. They were not officially pardoned until 2013, by which stage most of them (including my father) were dead.

Many returning servicemen, some with glittering war records, were treated with hostility by the local population, but my father always told me he was never shown anything other than friendliness. Donegal, because of its predominantly Catholic population, was one of only three of the nine Ulster counties that joined the Irish Free State (later the Republic of Ireland) after Partition in 1921, and some of my mother's family, and many of the neighbours, must have been staunch Republicans. But they never took it out on my father for joining the British army. The loss of benefits meant nothing to him – he was settled in England by that point, where the benefits were much better (Ireland didn't get a national health service until much later) and there were no jobs in Donegal. I don't think he ever considered going back to live in Ireland. Other than their regular summer holidays in Donegal, my parents spent the rest of their lives in England and are buried there.

Unlike the farm-cottage where my mother was born in Donegal, the council house in Leeds had a basic but modern kitchen with a cooker, running hot and cold water, an indoor lavatory, a bath and electricity that worked. It wasn't much, but it was a step up for both of them. My father got a job on the shop floor of a factory owned by Yorkshire Copper Works, a large local company that made copper and brass tubes for boilers and the plumbing industry. Initially, he had no skills so was paid very little, and my mother must have struggled to feed her family, which kept on getting bigger. My brother Johnnie was born in 1946, and I came along in February 1948, the third of what would ultimately be their six children. Peter, Margaret and Philip followed me with roughly two years between each of us.

My father was a hard worker and when he moved up to semi-skilled status things became a bit easier. But I was in my teens by then – in my early childhood he barely earned enough to feed his family.

When I first read Frank McCourt's book *Angela's Ashes*, the tragic story of a poor family growing up in a slum in Limerick, it brought back memories of my own upbringing. The mother in the book, Angela, is an extraordinarily brave lady who, despite a criminally irresponsible and permanently drunk husband, the death of three children and grinding poverty, never lowers her expectations for her sons and raises them to be well-behaved, conscientious and hardworking people. My mother had similar expectations for us all and never compromised her standards, no matter how poor we were. She was a brave and good woman.

We were never quite as poor as the family in *Angela's Ashes*, and my father, unlike the drunken, cruel father in *Angel's Ashes*, was never violent. But there were similarities: we four boys slept in the same bed, alternately head to toe, my two sisters shared a small box room and my parents had their own bedroom. My father's wages, peanuts in the early years of his marriage, were barely enough to go round and one question that was never asked in our house was, 'What would you like for your tea?' You ate what was put on the table. But we never went hungry – there was always enough to eat, even if it was just bread and butter, which it often was.

Clothes got handed down and to make them last longer my mother made me wear some of my sister's old clothes. She wanted the other boys to wear them too but gave up when they started wailing, 'I'm not wearing a girl's cardie to school.' But I wasn't bothered. From an early age, I could handle myself, and I was never afraid of a fight, so no one dared jeer at me.

In wintertime our bedroom got so cold that our breath froze on the windows and my mother used to buy old coats to put on our beds because they were cheaper than blankets.

She used to put us in the bath in order of age, oldest first, and then send us downstairs to dry ourselves in front of the coal fire, which had no fireguard. Johnnie, as the eldest boy, was always first into the bath and I followed him. One day, when I was about six, I was just getting into the bath when there was a loud screaming from below and my mother raced down to find Johnnie literally ablaze. He had got too close to the flames and his pyjamas had caught fire. She wrapped him in a rug and got a neighbour to run to the shops and phone for an ambulance. He was taken to St James' Hospital and was not expected to live.

The social services people came around the next day to see my mother and warned her that if something like that happened again, they would take the rest of us into care. She had a bit of a reputation by then, and was told in no uncertain terms that she was an irresponsible mother and should not light a naked fire again without a fireguard – which of course we couldn't afford. I listened in as usual, shocked by what I was hearing: however bad conditions were at home, they were a lot better than the care homes I had heard about. But I was even more worried about my brother Johnnie. He stayed in hospital for ten months and when he finally came home he was very different to the cheerful, happy brother I had known. He was never the same again.

That house, 25 Throstle Hill, was not a lucky one for us. I was still a young lad when my eldest sister Kathleen began to go off the rails. At the age of eleven, she left St Philip's Primary School expecting to go to St Francis Girls Catholic in Holbeck, a half-hour's bus ride away, which was a grammar school with a good academic record. But for some reason my mother said 'no' and sent her to the secondary modern at the top of our street. She was a bright kid, and it was totally wrong for her. I can still remember the priest coming to the house and telling my mother off, but she refused to relent. She hated being pushed around by the priests.

At the age of fourteen Kathleen began coming home late and when my mother asked her where she had been, she always said the school Youth Club. That sounded harmless enough but my mother became suspicious and told my dad to go up there and see what she was up to. Although I was only a lad of eight, he brought me along. We found the Youth Club leader who told us that our Kathleen had not been there for months.

When Kathleen came home that evening and said she had been at the Youth Club, there was a huge row. My mother gave her a good hiding and from that moment on they were at each other's throats. It was a very small house and the atmosphere at home was poisonous.

Eventually, Kathleen, still a teenager, left home without telling anyone, and my mother never mentioned her name again. She simply dropped out of our lives, as if she had never been. It was only years later, by which point I was better off and wanted to help, that I found out what had happened to her. It was tragic. After leaving home, she went to my aunt's house in London where she got seriously into drugs and goodness knows what else. I think my aunt probably threw her out and she married an East End 'Jack the Lad', with whom she had three children in quick succession. She left him for a Turkish drug dealer, and they were eventually caught trying to smuggle a consignment of drugs through Heathrow. They were both sent to jail, and she served time in Styal Prison in Cheshire. Soon after she came out, she overdosed on heroin and died. Poor thing. Born in a slum in war-time England, deprived of her mother for the first three years of her life, sent to the wrong school, cut off by her own mother, a drug addict from her teenage years — she never had a chance. Sometimes I look at her picture with the rest of us and can't believe all of that happened to her. I did track down her children and did my best for them, but I wished I could have done more for my sister when she was alive.

All this paints a picture of uncaring parents, but that wasn't so. I thought then, and I think now, that I could not have had better parents. My father was a lovely, hard-working man, liked by everyone, and respected by us. He hadn't a bad bone in his body, and he was always very good to us, playing games or taking us to the cinema or to watch football (my life-long support for Leeds United dates from that time). I discovered afterwards that he had actually been a very good footballer and played for the (Irish) army; he was also a champion table tennis player. But he never spoke about it, just as he never talked much about his childhood or his years in the army. He spent his wages on his family and his one extravagance was a visit to the St Joseph's Catholic Club in Hunslet on a Saturday night when a lot of beer was consumed. Someone once told me that my father could drink ten points of beer in an evening and sometimes more. But I never saw him drink during the week, and the odd occasion that he came home drunk he was never violent or abusive — just happy.

At home there was no question of who was the boss: my mother ruled the roost. We didn't have a dog but somehow she had acquired a dog lead and if you did something wrong, or created extra expense by tearing your trousers or breaking a precious mug or plate, she'd whack you with it. She saw it as the best way to keep us out of mischief and, on the whole, she was right. If she did it today, she'd probably have the children taken away by a social worker, but that was accepted as the norm then and we were probably hit less than many of the others in the street.

The older I get, the more I appreciate her. You could say that my parents failed with my sister Kathleen or by not taking basic precautions to protect Johnnie, but a good whack with that dog lead kept the rest of us in line, and I don't think it did us any harm. I understand her better now, but my brothers and sister don't and sometimes I wonder if we grew up in the same household. My work ethic and principles definitely came from my mother who, despite her lack of education and circumstances, loved art and music – as I do. She was fiercely independent and never felt anyone was better than her – characteristics she passed on to me, too. I think lots of people were in awe of her.

Like so many people of their generation, my parents were not big on emotion, and I can't ever remember being hugged or kissed by either of them. But there was a tender side to my mother that she never liked to show. She would always tuck us in every night and the next morning we would find our clothes, washed and ironed, in a neat pile at the end of bed. She must have stayed up until the early hours, polishing our shoes and getting everything ready for school the next day. I never polished my own shoes until after I left home at seventeen – my mother always did that for me.

At Christmas time she would say, 'I'm too busy to do presents this year. Here's a pound each. Go buy your own,' and we would travel into town and spend it, probably in Woolworths where it went a lot further. There was no question of a Christmas tree or decorations, but we'd have a big dinner in the middle of the day on Christmas Day, with chicken rather than turkey. We couldn't afford turkey.

Yet we were better off than many of the other residents in our street. There were children with the bottoms hanging out of their trousers, living in filthy houses with little to eat. I knew a family down the road whose mother had run away and their father was a drunk who was never in, so they lived in squalor. They never washed their clothes and used to sit on orange boxes and drink their tea out of jam jars. Yet it was in their house that I first saw a television. How they acquired the set, I have no idea, but it was the first television (black-and-white of course) in the street, and we would all go round and watch it. We didn't get our own TV until I was thirteen and had moved into our own house.

We were usually up to some kind of mischief, fairly harmless stuff, but enough to get us into trouble. There was an old factory down the road that had closed some years earlier, and one day our little gang, including my brother Philip, found a door that had been left open and we ventured inside. It used to make rubber bands and there were abandoned piles of them all over the factory floor. We began making rubber balls and throwing them at one another, probably making a lot of noise. All of a sudden, this big fat guy with an Alsatian dog appeared and shouted, 'What are you lot doing in here?' He lined us up against the wall and demanded to know who we were.

We all gave false names and addresses, but my little brother, terrified of the dog, gave the game away. 'My name is Philip Adderley and I'm *his* brother,' he said, pointing at me. I had given the name of Jones or something, but poor Philip, half an eye on the dog, gave him the correct name and address.

'I'm going to see your mother about this,' the man threatened. 'Now clear off.' Philip and I ran home and quickly told my mother about the man and the dog.

'We weren't doing anything wrong,' I pleaded. 'Just playing. He said he's coming around to see you.'

We just had time to get our story in before a car drove up and stopped outside our little gate. There was a knock on the door and my mother opened it to be confronted with the fat guy and his dog. 'What do you want?' she demanded aggressively, catching him off guard. When he began to complain about us breaking into the factory, she went back into the house and came out with a broom. She whacked him with it, good and hard, shouting, 'Don't you ever touch my kids or threaten them with your dog again! Now get out of here!' He jumped into his car, and we never saw him or his dog again.

My mother was quite fearless, refusing to be intimidated by anyone. On one occasion, I had to bring her a note from one of the teachers at school with the curt message: 'I WANT TO SEE YOU ABOUT YOUR WILLIAM.' She simply turned it over and wrote on the back: 'YOU KNOW WHERE I LIVE!' and sent it back. He never followed up on it – he knew when he'd met his match.

Money was always tight, and we got up to every possible scheme to help out. My brothers and I did a paper round every morning, getting up at the crack of dawn before going to school. Once a week, with some of the other lads, I used to go around our area asking people if they had any empty bottles they couldn't be bothered returning to get their deposit back. Tizer bottles were the best as they fetched threepence each, and the shop at the top of the road, aware they were dealing with families who didn't have much, usually took them from us. Sometimes they put them out the back and we would nip around, collect them and bring them in again.

At Christmas time my three brothers and I used to go carol singing, taking one street each. Most of the people would say 'clear off' and we would move on but there was always the odd house that would give you a couple of shillings. We'd swap information when we got back home and the next night the other brothers would go to what we called 'the good houses' where there was more of a chance of getting something.

Another fund-raising scheme was the 'pigswill round'. On Sunday afternoons after dinner, I would take my dad's wheelbarrow down the street collecting the leftovers that I would then take round to the allotment and sell for sixpence a barrow. We each had our separate rounds and once you looked after a certain house, they would keep things for you.

Our little gang also found a way of raiding the local co-op where they stored the milk brought in on the milk floats. The bottles were stored in a cold room protected by iron bars but one of the boys, who wasn't so well fed, was so thin he could squeeze through and pass out bottles of milk and orange juice, which we took home. My mother gratefully received them and never asked us where they came from.

We were constantly hungry, and I remember one day I found a chicken that someone had dropped on the road and ran home to give it my mother. It fed the whole family for two days. On another occasion I found a packet of cigarettes and gave them to my dad.

The outskirts of Leeds were surrounded by farms and my mother would sometimes say, 'Go down to the fields and fetch us some turnips,' and we would go and help ourselves to whatever vegetables were within reach, warily watching for the farmer. Rhubarb grew in profusion around Leeds and when it was in season we almost lived off it; in the autumn we raided the apple orchards, mostly taking the apples that had fallen on the ground.

We were poor but I don't remember as a boy ever feeling really poor. Everybody at school lived like we did – or worse – and we felt no different to anyone else. That's how things were on a big council estate, and it never bothered me. I sometimes think that even now I could go back and live there and it would feel just normal.

★★★★★

Unlike my grandparents in Donegal, we were not religious, but we seldom missed Sunday mass at St Philip's Church. It was a serious matter: on Monday mornings the teachers would ask you whether you had been to mass, and it was entered into a register. For a time, I was a dutiful young lad and became an altar boy, chanting my responses to the priest in Latin, which I knew by heart. I learned how to swing the incense censer, present the bread and the wine to the priest for holy communion and solemnly pour the holy water for him to ritually wash his hands at the side of the altar, murmuring, *'Lava me, Domine'* ('Lord, wash away my iniquity'). Other than the need to get up early on Sunday mornings, I quite enjoyed the ritual, and I can still recite some of those Latin responses more than sixty years later.

I was about nine when I learned an invaluable lesson that served me well for the rest of my life. On my way home every day, I had to pass the Protestant school where every so often I got into a fight with some of the boys. We were all from the same working-class background and there was nothing factional about it, although they liked to call us 'Catalites' and we called them 'Proddy-dogs'. It was mostly harmless but there was a big lad, several years older than me, who picked on me. He would block my way home and demand, 'Have you got any money on you? Any sweets?' If I had nothing, which was most of the time, he'd punch me.

After one particularly bruising encounter I went home and told my father, 'There's a Protestant boy at the top of the road, and every time I pass the school, he hits me for no reason.'

I thought my father would go up there the next day and sort him out. But not a bit of it. 'Well, hit him back then. What do you want me to do about it?' The next day, when the boy hit me, I hit him back and he never touched me again.

Later on in life, I found that there's always someone who will try to bully you, in business as well as school, and I discovered at an early stage the importance of standing up for yourself and giving back as much as you get. On the whole I like to think I am a mild-mannered, benign and peaceable man (although there are those who probably don't agree), but I do have an Irish temper when I'm riled. I learned at an early age that you have to look after yourself – no one else will.

★★★★★

MY FATHER

I was about twelve when things began to look up. One day my father came home with his latest pay slip, which he proudly showed me. He had been promoted and that week he had earned £25, which he thought was riches. He was on a roll and soon after that he bought a nice little semi at the top end of Middleton – I seem to remember he paid £1,800 for it, with the help of a mortgage – with a garden where he spent most of his weekends. It was directly opposite Middleton Park, a magical area of green with a lake where you could go boating, fishing, play tennis or even bowls, and there were woods at the back where we could play. It was a big step up from the council house, although I still slept in a bed with my brothers.

Chapter 3

School Days

I left school in 1964, aged sixteen, with four O-Levels – maths, English, geography, and technical drawing – good enough to get a job but I know I could have done much better. Unfortunately, I never really took to school and, with one or two exceptions, never liked or respected the teachers – sentiments that were probably mutual.

I started my education at St Philip's Catholic Junior Primary where my abiding memory is of performing on the stage, which was one of the few things I was good at in my school days. We had a wonderful teacher, Mrs Briggs, who took a liking to me and said I had a natural talent and should go on the stage. I was given parts in productions by some of the senior classes. I had no stage fright and in later life, when I had to make a speech, I never had a problem standing up in front of an audience.

Mrs Briggs encouraged me to study for the eleven-plus and go on to St Michael's Catholic College, a boys-only grammar school run by the Jesuits. The problem was you had to wear a uniform, and we couldn't afford one. If you failed, you went to St Joseph's Catholic Secondary School, a much tougher school whose only advantage was that they didn't require uniforms. My elder brother had failed the eleven-plus, and I failed it too – and, much to Mrs Briggs' disappointment, I followed my brother to St Joseph's.

Two years later I moved to Corpus Christi Secondary, a comprehensive school where I never excelled at anything in the three years I was there. I loved sport and for a while I fancied myself as a boxer, until I lost to a guy who absolutely hammered me. His name was Albert Yates and there was nothing on him, just bones, and I could tell I was never going to hurt him no matter how hard I hit him. I looked at him as he was getting into the ring, mesmerised by his bony fists that were about twice the size of mine. He gave me such a beating that I never entered the ring again.

My football career didn't last long either. My position was goalkeeper, and I was doing all right until a lad called Ken Robinson joined the school. He could kick the ball further down the pitch than me, which for some reason impressed the teacher much more than my ability to keep the ball out of the net. So I was dropped and he was put in goal and I didn't get another game after that. It never occurred to the teacher – or me – that I could play in another position.

I started off loving English but the English teacher, a man called George Quirk, didn't love me. He was a big guy, who also coached the school rugby league team, and he would physically fight with students in the classroom. I remember he elbowed one guy in the face. Perhaps because I stood up to him and didn't play rugby, he picked on me at every lesson, taking the mickey out of my homework and bringing me up to the front of the class or hitting me for no reason. I soon lost all enthusiasm for English.

My schoolmates were a great bunch of lads, and I made many friends, but I never settled at Corpus Christi and felt more and more oppressed at school as time wore on. I don't blame the teachers for that, although they were not very inspiring. The exception was the maths teacher, Arthur Aldridge, from whom I learned more than all the others put together. In later years, when I was running a stall in Leicester market, I had to be good at mental arithmetic and I was, working out quite complicated sums in my head at high speed.

My problem at school was that I just didn't see the point of it all: why should we study chemistry or physics when there was no prospect that any of the lads would ever use them? I just thought, 'Well, what am I learning here? I can read, I can write, I can do maths. What more do I want?' I still hold that view, unfashionable as it is today. Why teach a lad of fifteen, whose mum and dad are living in abject poverty, subjects like chemistry or physics when they know full well it is not going to help them get a job? Most of my classmates ended up working in a warehouse or on the factory floor. I still feel they should have been teaching them the practical things of life, preparing them for the world they were actually going to have to live in. None of us ever became scientists.

Oddly enough my younger sister and my brothers, who also went to Corpus Christi, got on fine with the teachers. My brother Peter, the cleverest of the six of us, did so well that he went on to Leeds University where he got a first in economics and later founded a very successful recruitment company.

Yet for all my lack of enthusiasm for school, I emerged as a self-confident, independent young man, with no feeling of resentment or inferiority, able to mix with anyone on my own terms.

Chapter 4

Woolworths – the Great Days

I was sixteen when I slept in my own bed for the first time. It wasn't much of a bed, more a bunk in a cheap boarding house in Hull where there must have been about fourteen single beds in the same room. It was the cheapest I could find but, after sleeping four to a bed all my life, I thought it was marvellous.

I had never been away from home before, and I was both excited and apprehensive in equal measure. I was a trainee manager at Woolworths, transferred to the branch in Hull where I had arrived earlier in the day to start work. I had no place to sleep so here I was in this hostel with my own bed.

I had begun my Woolworths' career in my home town of Leeds in 1963, aged fifteen, as a 'Saturday boy', working one day a week. I was desperate to earn some money, and someone told me that the Woolworths store on Briggate, in the centre of Leeds, was taking on youngsters to work on Saturdays after school. I took the bus down-town, entered the crowded store, found my way to the office and simply asked a lady, 'Have you got any jobs?' She had, and within an hour I was working on the slab cake counter, carrying boxes of cake from the stockroom to the sales floor where half a dozen girls of varying ages cut the slabs into wedges, weighed them on scales and served them to the customer.

My job was to keep the counter supplied with cake, which was delivered to the stockroom during the week. The trainee manager in charge of the counter told me what cake they wanted – 'five slabs of cherry Genoa, four of angel cake, six Madeira' and so on – and I would rush upstairs, open the large boxes, load up my barrow, take the lift down to the food market on the first floor and push my way through the throng of shoppers, shouting, 'Mind your backs, mind your backs! Excuse me, excuse me. Can I get through?'

It went on all afternoon, up and down to the stockroom, opening boxes, loading up the barrow and racing down again, all the time trying to keep up with the pace at which the cake was going out the door. I was a quick learner and soon got to know the names of the different kinds of cake, and which ones sold best, essential when I had to load up my barrow in the stockroom.

On my first day I was told in no uncertain terms that I was not allowed to sit down, even if we had no customers – I had to make myself look busy at all times, so when I wasn't doing anything else, I swept the floors. The luxury of having no customers never arose on a Saturday, but there were times when I would have loved to have been on my own.

Nothing, however, could take away from the pleasure and pride of working for the great Woolworths group. I find it difficult now to explain to younger people how important Woolworths was for the British shopper. It was an institution, part of the country's fabric, its distinctive red-and-cream-fronted stores the centre-piece of the high street in every big town. In its heyday (which was roughly the period 1930 to 1965), it was arguably the most successful retail format ever created. Everyone, young and old, rich and poor, shopped at Woolworths, some of the women often dressing up on Saturdays, the big day.

The company's claim – and it was true – was that it was the biggest retailer of almost everything the British consumer wanted to buy. It sold more sweets, more toys, more shoes, more hardware and just about everything else – including, as I saw for myself on that first day, cake – than any retailer in the country. It was basically the whole high street in one place, selling a vast range of good quality goods, from food, toiletries and toys, to clothing, household goods and gardening tools, offering value for money that no other store could compete with. It was the shop where as kids we spent our pocket money on pick 'n' mix sweets and never missed the toy department at Christmas time when they always had a new range of mechanical toys that we could only drool over. I got my first fishing rod there, which I took to Donegal every year, and my first football boots. My mother bought her needles and thread there to repair our clothes and my father, a keen gardener, bought his gardening tools from Woolworths.

There was something for everyone, whatever their age or interests. In my teenage years, it was Britain's biggest music retailer and sold millions of records – cheaper versions of hit singles – under its own label, Embassy Records. My friends and I used to spend hours in the music department in the basement listening to the Beatles and the latest hit pop songs, which played on the speakers all day. Occasionally – very occasionally in my case – we would buy a record, a 45 rpm vinyl disc, to take home.

On Saturdays the stores were so packed that children often got lost and there were regular announcements asking anxious mothers to come to the lost property desk to collect their little ones. Parents would often make their children stand outside, because the store was so packed inside they feared for their safety.

Many people assumed that Woolworths was as British as fish and chips, but it was actually an American company, founded by Frank Winfield Woolworths in 1879 as a 'five and dime' store, which meant that everything cost either 5 cents or 10 cents. It opened its first British store in Liverpool in 1909, changing the 'five-and-dime' to 'threepence and sixpence' (3d and 6d) with 6d the upper limit for any item in the store. In my childhood, old-timers still talked about the store motto of 'nothing over 6d'. When Frank Woolworth died in 1919 his epitaph was: 'He made his money not by selling a little for a lot, but by selling a lot for a little.'

The British company boomed and by the mid-1930s it was opening a new store every five days, passing 600 by 1934 and 1,000 by 1958. Woolworths was the only stores group included in the original (1935) *Financial Times* 30-share index and by the late 1950s was the second biggest company quoted on the London Stock Exchange after the mighty *ICI*.

Briggate, where I started out, was the fifth store that Woolworths built in Britain (officially it was known as 'Leeds 5') and the second biggest in the country. It originally opened in 1910, and I am just old enough to remember its re-opening, after an extensive rebuilding, in 1959 as one of Woolworths first 'superstores', which is how it was in my time. I remember well its imposing double staircase that led to the lower ground floor; it also had one of the very first escalators, a novel feature in the 1950s on which we children loved to ride up and down until my mother stopped us.

When I joined in 1964 Woolworth's greatest days were almost over, although very few people understood that until much later. New, more fashionable retailers such as Marks & Spencer, British Home Stores, and Mothercare were chipping away at its market, and Woolworth got stuck at the bottom end in the 1960s and 1970s when shoppers were becoming more prosperous. It completely lost its way and, although it belatedly embraced the trend to out-of-town shopping, it made a hash of it and had to close the operation down.

As a 'Saturday boy' carrying cake up and down in the lift, I didn't know any of this of course. But I did know that working for Woolworth was what I wanted to do, and I was determined to make a go of it. I didn't get paid much, but it was welcome money, and I enjoyed the work. Working for Woolworths was like joining a huge, friendly family, every member loyal to their paternalistic employer who in turn looked after them remarkably well.

The cake counter was watched over by a trainee manager and at the start I set my sights on being like him. Trainee managers were really glorified floorwalkers, but they fancied themselves as being a cut above the rest of the staff, destined to be the next generation of managers to run the stores, maybe even getting to be chairman one day. There were about a dozen of them in Briggate and they always seemed to be good-looking and cocky, with slicked-back hair, dark suits, smart collar and tie and an air of authority well beyond their years. The company's policy, rigidly enforced, was that every member of the management team, right up to the chairman, started off by sweeping the floors and worked their way up step by step. There were no shortcuts. Trainee manager was the first rung on the ladder. 'Saturday boy' wasn't even on the ladder.

The trainee with responsibility for the cake counter was Bob Marshall, only a year or two older than me, who I tried to impress with my eagerness and speed around the place. I must have succeeded because after I had been there for about three months he took me aside and said, 'Right, I'm going to give you another job. I can't be bothered ordering the cake every Saturday night. You can do it before you go home.' At which point, *he* went home, leaving me to get on with it. That was typical of Woolworths' training at the time: you were thrown in at the deep end and learned on the job.

In this case it wasn't difficult. Cake was ordered from the suppliers, Southport Cakes of Manchester and Knightsbridge Cake, every Saturday after the store closed and was delivered over the following week. Everything was neatly laid out on the order form, and you just had to fill in the amount you wanted. I went back into the stockroom and counted the boxes of each variety we had left and checked how many had originally been ordered. For instance, last week's order might have been for ten boxes of angel layer cake and only two were left – which meant I had to order eight, maybe nine to be on the safe side. I worked my way down the list, completed the form, put it in an envelope and posted it to Southport Cakes. They would get it on Monday morning and deliver the cakes from Wednesday onwards.

After that, Bob let me spend more of my time working on the cake counter, initially taking over from the regular staff when they needed a break or when the store became too busy for them to keep up. I soon became expert at it. Before the

The cottage in Donegal where my mother was born in 1923. It had no electricity, no indoor lavatory, no stove and no running water. Left: this is me as a boy fetching water for my grandmother.

Far left: My grandparents, Katie and Will Gill, around the open turf fire where my grannie did all her cooking and baking. Left: my grandparents as I remember them. They were the oldest married couple in Ireland.

Above: the cottage as it is today.

Helping Grandad on his farm in Donegal. I am on his right with my brothers Peter (dark jacket) and Johnnie (back left). My sister Margaret is on the right of the picture. Right top: me with two of my three brothers, Peter (left) and Johnnie (centre). Right: my eldest brother Johnnie in school cap and suit that my mother bought second-hand.

Above left: my grandparents with my wife Jean and my cousins in Donegal; and right, four of us with my parents. I am sitting on my father's knee.

All six Adderley children in our council house in Leeds. From the left: Philip, the youngest, born in 1954; Peter (1950); Johnnie ((1946), at the front centre); me, born in 1948; and my younger sister Margaret (1952) on the right of the picture. The eldest, Kathleen (born in 1942), is at the back. She was to have a tragic life.

Above: Jean's parents, George and Betty Thornton. Right: my paternal grandmother, my father's mother, who was from Dublin where my father was born.

Above left: courting Jean with my precious mini, my first car, in the background. Right: the happy couple on honeymoon. Below: our wedding day, 20th September 1969. Jean was a Methodist and I was a Catholic so a priest and a Methodist minister jointly presided over the service.

Our first house, a lovely cottage in Elton, near Peterborough, which we rented. Our first child, Theresa, was born there but tragically died when she was only six months old.

Bottom: our two boys, Will, right, and Jonathan.

Where it all began: my first stall in Leicester Market, which I opened in December 1979. At that time, it was the biggest covered market in Europe and had been on the same site for 700 years. It is currently undergoing a multi-million pound refurbishment.

Photo: *Alamy*

Below left, in 1986, seven years after I started my little business, I bought an old foundry in Churchgate, right in the heart of Leicester, and it became Dunelm's first shop. The Rex Cinema in Coalville followed a year later.

Today Dunelm has 184 modern stores and is now the market leader in homeware in the UK with sales of £1.7 billion and profits of more than £200m. The stock market value is more than £2 billion and the Adderley family are still the biggest shareholders.

Dunelm's modern head office (above) and distribution centre (below) in Fosse Way, Syston, just outside Leicester. We opened our first, much more modest, head office on the same site in 1995.

One of Dunelm's fleet of modern trucks. I started the business in 1979 with one old bread van I bought for £200.

My official portrait taken when I was appointed manager of my first Woolworth store (872 Ladypool Road, Birmingham) in 1968. I was twenty.

Below, the grandest house Jean and I ever owned, Thornhaugh Hall, near Stamford. It had 300 acres of land, a lake with its own boathouse, spacious gardens and a stable courtyard.

We sold it after twelve years. Been there, done that!

Thornhaugh Hall Estate
Photo: *Shutterstock*

days of self-service, which came in a few years later, there used to be big slabs of cake laid out on the counter and a customer would walk up and say, for example, 'I want half a pound of cherry Genoa,' and you'd cut it by eye, put it on the scales and work out the exact price.

After a while I didn't even have to use the scales: I could cut the exact amount every time and no one queried the price. 'That'll be one and six,' I'd tell the customer. I knew all the varieties we sold – chocolate sponge, mocha sponge, even 'unfilled sponge', which customers would take away to use as a base for a birthday cake, adding their own ingredients and topping.

I did that for a year, working every Saturday, and full-time in the school holidays, all the time learning the trade, absorbing information like one of the unfilled sponges we sold in the store. In one year, I physically grew four inches, gaining in self-confidence and assurance all the time. I sat fretting in school all week, just going through the motions, impatient for Saturday lunch-time to arrive when I could catch the bus down-town.

After about six months at the store I found a girlfriend, my first. Her name was Elizabeth and she worked Saturdays like me, giving me yet another reason to look forward to the weekend. I was still living at home, sharing a bed with my brothers, and she was a good Catholic girl from Notre Dame Highschool for Girls, so there wasn't much opportunity to get beyond holding hands and the occasional goodnight kiss on her doorstep. She eventually dumped me for someone older – probably one of the trainee managers. Some of the excitement went out of Saturdays after that. Towards the end of my first year, someone in the personnel department handed me a little red booklet with the title 'A CAREER FOR YOU AT F. W. WOOLWORTH'. Its introduction read, 'If you are single, physically fit and not more than twenty-three years of age, are a graduate, have A Levels or four O Levels, write to the personnel manager.' It gave a Birmingham address.

I was single, fit, under twenty-four and was studying for four O-levels. I was in love with Woolworth by then and working there was all I wanted to do. So I applied for a job as a trainee manager, went for an interview, was accepted and I started work in September 1964, earning £5 a week.

Woolworth offered five-day courses in the company training centre at Castleton, Lancashire, but basically we trained on the job, working long hours, Monday to Saturday, picking up what we could as we went along. There were thirty-six departments in the superstores, and before you could become a manager you had to have managed all of them. You also had to master a wide range of disciplines, invaluable to me in later life when I had my own retail shops: stock control, counter and window display, staff relations, cash control, government regulations and even basic economics. It was a great training system and set me up for life.

Everything was done by hand: there were no computers, the tills didn't automatically add up and stock was physically counted and recorded in pencil in a stock book. Everything had to be checked and double-checked, finally by the manager himself who was responsible for everything – particularly discrepancies – at the end of the week.

Trainees had to dress smartly in dark suits and white shirts with separate collars. Marks & Spencer was one of the few stores that still sold collarless shirts and fortunately there was one next door. Woolworths itself had a line of stiff paper collars that could be reversed when they got dirty but we preferred the M&S ones.

The management held firmly to the view that Woolworths was the only truly professional retailer in the country and the others were just amateurs playing at being shopkeepers. One store manager was heard to boast that he could 'run Marks & Spencer in my lunch hour'. That was the Woolworths culture, which was drilled into us trainees and we believed it at the time. Later, when M&S overtook us to become the biggest retailer in the country, we changed our minds – but it was too late by then.

Even though women made up 80 per cent of the group's 200,000 employees countrywide, all the top positions in the company were occupied by men and there were very few female trainee managers or managers in my time (in fact I don't remember any). Most stores had a canteen that provided a cooked breakfast but men didn't eat with women and managers ate separately in their own dining room.

When I started out as a Saturday boy, becoming a trainee manager was as far as my imagination or ambitions went. But once I had achieved that, I raised my sights to becoming a manager, and somewhere along the way I decided to aim for the very top: one day I would become the chairman of the whole company, king of all I surveyed. For the next fourteen years that was what drove me, causing me to push myself far beyond the call of duty. I gave it everything I'd got, working six-day weeks, soaking up information as I went along, always trying to out-pace my less ambitious colleagues, and trying to make my store, wherever it was, the most profitable in the group. I always believed, even at school, that I could do anything.

The manager of the Leeds store in my time was an extraordinary man called Charlie Beck who was a legend across the group. Even board members in London treated him with respect, most unusual in Woolworths, and the buyers, the real power at Woolworths, were terrified of him. Managers got a share of the profits and Charlie was probably the highest paid man in the company, including the chairman in far-off London, and was even rumoured to own a castle in Spain.

He ruled over Briggate with a benign but firm hand from an office on the first floor that a former employee once described as 'like the bridge on a ship overlooking the ground sales floor' (there were three floors at Briggate). He was a great motivator, and the staff would do anything for him – which helped explain his success. I learned a lot from him.

Most of the group merchandise managers and buyers drove Jaguars or Humber Super Snipes, which the trainees often had to park for them. But Charlie drove a van that was used to deliver bulkier items to customers after the store closed, a service provided by no other store in the group or high street chain for that matter. I was too young to have a driving licence, but the older trainees were roped in as delivery drivers, which they regarded as a privilege. Charlie would go to any lengths to increase sales.

I had been working at Briggate full-time for six months when I got my first leg up the management ladder. I was called to the office one day and told, 'You've been promoted. You're going to Hull as a trainee.' The system they had then was to move trainees, American-style, around the country at the drop of a hat, which for a seventeen-year-old living at home was disconcerting to say the least. It was actually a reward for the good work I had done, but I didn't see it that way at the time. Even senior managers, as I discovered later, could suddenly find themselves posted to some distant and inconvenient place, regardless of whether their wives and children wanted to go. I was single, with no ties, but I really didn't want to go either.

Most trainees were given a week's notice of a transfer, which gave them a bit of time to get themselves together, but I was told they needed me in Hull by lunchtime the next day. When I asked about digs, I was told, 'Just go, that's it, that's your problem.' One of the first lessons Woolworths taught you was that you had to stand on your own two feet and rely on yourself.

When I got home that evening I told my parents that they wanted me to go to Hull. 'When?' asked my mother.

'Tomorrow.' She was furious.

'You're not going,' she said. 'You're too young.'

My father was more pragmatic. 'Look, if he's going to make a career of it, he's got to go.'

So I set off the next morning with no idea of where I would stay or even what I would do.

I arrived in the Hull store at lunchtime and reported for duty, half-expecting them to say, 'Take the rest of the day off and get yourself sorted out.' But they didn't. They put me to work straight away, and it was only after the store closed that I could go out and find a place to stay. Someone must have given me an address because I ended up in this room with more than a dozen others – and my own bed for the first time.

I was tired after a long and stressful day and, after carefully hanging up my precious suit, I was just falling off to sleep when a noisy group of building workers – I think they were plasterers from Bradford – staggered in from the pub. For the next two hours they laughed and joked and made such a noise that sleep was out of the question. Finally, at about one in the morning, I said, rather tentatively, 'Excuse me, but I've got to go to work tomorrow. I have to be there at eight. Do you mind if I get some sleep?'

There was silence, and I thought, 'I'm for it now.' One of them remarked, 'Hello, we've got James Bond here,' but one of the older ones cut him short.

'Let the lad sleep,' he said. They went quiet after that, and I finally got some sleep. That was something else I learned that night: if you approached people in the right way, you could usually get them on your side.

Breakfast the next morning was provided by a guy who appeared with a kettle and a frying pan at the end of the room and cooked rashers and eggs, after which I left for the store. I soon found myself better accommodation, living with a family, and things improved after that.

I was given four departments to look after: the sweet counter, the biscuit counter, the bread counter and, of course, the cake counter. I had learned a lot in my time at Briggate, and at Hull I felt I could cope with anything they threw at me. My knowledge and my management skills expanded almost by the day. Once again, I worked very long hours, including weekends, and one of the managers told me I was already being seen as a promising young man, destined for higher things.

As soon as I could afford it, I took driving lessons, passed my test and bought my first car, a second-hand Mini. I was very proud of it and drove it back to Leeds to show my parents. Neither of them could drive, although I could see that my father was itching to learn. I started teaching him at weekends but he kept failing his test, complaining that the only car he could drive was my Mini that he was familiar with.

'Can't you take a week off and help me get me through my test?' he begged. I only got two weeks' holiday a year and time off was very precious, but he was so keen that I agreed. We practiced and practiced until the time came for him to take the test, which he insisted on doing in the Mini rather than the driving-school car, which is what most people did. Nervously I waved him off with the examiner. When he came back he looked pleased with himself. 'I've passed,' he said. 'But don't tell your mother.'

My father put on a sombre face in front of my mother and told her, 'I failed again.' For a moment I thought she was going to get the dog lead out, but then he admitted, 'No, I've passed. I'm only joking!' It was an important turning point for both of them. Britain was becoming more prosperous in the late 1960s and many of my parents' friends lived in their own houses with cars parked in the driveway. Cars, like television sets, were becoming an essential part of everyday middle-class life and they were feeling increasingly excluded and isolated. Eventually, they bought their own little car and went everywhere in it, very important as they got older.

Chapter 5

Manager

Woolworths had a thousand stores and a thousand managers and about 100 new ones were appointed each year. The rewards were legendary. Charlie Beck, with his fabled castle in Spain, was probably the richest of them, but the manager of Belfast, who was said to have his own private zoo, was among several leading contenders for the title.

There were many more trainees than there were managers and only about one in ten would make it to the top. I was on a very steep learning curve and in those early days in Hull I had to dig deep and find out everything about all the departments under my control in a very short space of time. Trainee managers didn't do any serving: we had the shop girls to do that. We did the ordering and made sure the items we were promoting that week were on prominent display: 'I want fruitcake on the counter there, not layer cake,' I would say to one of the girls, or it would be: 'We want you to feature ginger biscuits this week.'

Every department was different, and I learned something new from each one. Crockery and glassware was particularly complex and I would have struggled without the support of the crockery supervisor, a kindly lady who had been with Woolworths for forty years. It was she who showed me some of the pitfalls that awaited the unwary. For instance, crockery was sold in sets of twelve and in my first week I ordered a full set of Cottage Design: twelve cups, twelve saucers, twelve tea plates and twelve dinner plates. That was wrong. Cups, she instructed me, broke much more often than saucers and had to be replaced. So I learned to order twelve saucers but eighteen cups. It was a simple thing, but important, and there were many more lessons like that.

There was a deep well of knowledge and experience in the store, and people were prepared to share it – as long as you asked in the right way. I always did and in turn was treated with great generosity by nice people who accepted me as part of the extended Woolworths' family. Several of the shop girls had worked for the group for more than thirty years and someone once told me that her parents had met when they were both employed in the store and she and her husband had done the same. It was a good place to work in those days.

After six months, I was given another six departments to manage and, as I gained experience, more departments were added. The system was that you eventually moved up from trainee to become an assistant manager of a smaller store, then deputy manager of a superstore and, finally, before full-time manager to temporary manager, covering holiday relief at another branch. Within a year, I had been promoted to deputy manager and moved on to another store, this time to Redcar, a seaside town on the Yorkshire coast. It was one of the smaller stores, so I took charge when the manager was on holiday or away. I was still only eighteen, less than two years into the job, but I felt I was moving fast up the ladder.

Managing a Woolworths store was a complex and challenging job, and there was a great deal to learn. But, in truth, the group ran like a well-oiled machine, with systems developed over many years designed to deal with every contingency. Everyone knew their jobs and carried them out efficiently and without fuss, although as manager you had to keep a watchful eye on every detail. During the day the cashiers went around and emptied the tills, and took the cash back to the office to be counted (cheques were very rare and credit cards non-existent). It was the cashier's responsibility to make sure it all added up and there was no fiddling going on at the tills, so every penny had to be reconciled at the end of each day and again at the end of the week. Shop-lifting was not the problem then that it is today, but managers had to plan for a degree of 'shrinkage' and sense that something was going wrong when the figure crept up.

I still retain – or fancy I do – some of the skills I picked up in my early days at Woolworths. Even today, I can de-bone a side of bacon, which I learned on the meat counter in Redcar in case the butcher didn't turn up (which sometimes he didn't); I became expert on cheeses from working in the deli in Coventry; I could run a café, if I had to, because we had a café in most of the stores; and I can even bake bread because we had in-house bakeries. I could take over a chain of shoe shops, or a chain of charity shops, or a chain of bargain shops or butcher shops, and know instinctively how to run them. As it happens, I ran a chain of homeware shops, and I learned the rudiments of how to do it in my time at Woolworths.

I also learned the importance of respecting the people who worked for me or with whom I came into contact. I always tell my grandchildren that it doesn't matter how clever, rich or successful you are, you must always treat other people with respect. I can't stand to see customers being rude to waiters or shop assistants just because they've got a lot of money.

In my first four years at Woolworth, I was moved six times: from Leeds I went to Hull, then Redcar, followed by Doncaster, Boston, Birmingham New Street, and Peterborough, where I was made deputy manager. I had just turned twenty when I got my first store as manager, which was Ladypool Road in Birmingham. There were actually more than forty Woolworths stores in Birmingham, the biggest of which was in the Bullring, about two miles away. Ladypool Road was one of the smaller ones, with just one floor of about 4,000 sq ft. Later, I would manage one of the biggest, West Bromwich, a superstore of 27,000 sq ft.

Ladypool was making a profit of £25,000 a year when I was appointed, and the deal I was offered gave me 10 per cent of the profit, a total, including my basic salary, of £3,600 a year, a decent enough wage in the late 1960s. But it was not enough for an ambitious young man rising in the world and from the moment I arrived I worked single-mindedly to drive up that figure, a task not made easy by the location of the store. Ladypool Road is in the famous Birmingham 'Balti Triangle' where the *balti*, a 'Pakistani Brummie' rice dish, was said to have been invented. It was one of the tougher parts of Birmingham, with a lot of immigrants and high unemployment and there was not much discretionary spending power. But if revenues were hard to increase, I decided I could do something about reducing costs. On my first day, I walked around the store, talking to the staff, trying to get the measure of the team and working out how I could make improvements and get the profits up.

The reward system at Woolworths was hugely skewed, with the managers often earning many times the next layer down. It was designed to incentivise managers, and, on the whole, it worked and managers moved heaven and earth to get their profits up. The downside of course was that if profits fell, not only did your earnings fall but you probably lost your job. I was keenly aware that if I had turned £25,000 profit into £20,000 or less, I would be out.

But in return Woolworths basically let you run your store as if it were your own, and as long as you made your numbers they pretty much left you alone. It was up to you to decide what you wanted to buy from the product list we received every week – within reason – and if you didn't like something you could reject it. You could choose your own staff and staff numbers, and you could decide where to save and where to spend money most profitably. Heating and lighting was an obvious area to save money, but there was obviously a limit and it had long been reached before I became a manager. I have already described how Charlie Beck increased the revenue at Briggate by using his own van to make deliveries and I knew one manager who even boiled his own ham and sold it in the store.

Soon after I arrived in Ladypool I walked around the outside of the building where I came across a window cleaner who was just starting work. My first thought was, 'I'm paying for 10 per cent of this guy's costs – personally.' So before he could climb up his ladder, I said to him: 'Excuse me. I've got some bad news for you. My area manager says we don't need a window cleaner. I'm sorry.'

I didn't have the guts to tell him it was my idea. To my relief, he just shrugged, muttered, 'Oh, well, never mind,' folded his ladder and pushed off. And then I started cleaning the windows myself. By the end of the year, I had turned £25,000 profit into £29,000, earning myself another £400.

I needed it, because by that stage I had a wife, a child and a mortgage.

Chapter 6

Jean

I first met Jean Thornton at Christmas time in 1967 when I was nineteen and she was twenty-one. I was out on the town with some friends, and we went to the Mecca Dance Hall in Leeds, as we sometimes did, in the hope that we might pick up one of the girls and generally enjoy ourselves. I saw this nice-looking girl across the floor, went over and asked her for a dance and we got chatting. We liked each other and she agreed to come on a date.

At the time I was the deputy manager of the Woolworths store in Redcar and fast-tracked for higher things, with a good salary and a car, and I was full of myself. To impress Jean with my worldliness and sophistication, I took her to the classiest restaurant I knew, the Berni Inn in Leeds.

Berni was a nationwide steak house chain that provided good food at reasonable prices and was very popular with people like me who had a few bob in their pocket. Their most popular meal was prawn cocktail followed by steak and chips, and that's what we both ordered. The place was crowded that night, and the waiters took an age, so we had plenty of time to exchange our family histories. She told me she came from the mining village of Kippax, on the outskirts of Leeds, but they weren't miners – her father was a commissionaire at the Burberry factory in Castleford, about three miles away, where Jean had been to the local grammar school. She lived with her parents, her two sisters and one brother on a council estate, not dissimilar to the one I grew up in. But unlike me, she had passed her eleven-plus, and got a place in Castleford Grammar School, which she could afford to attend only because she inherited her cousin's hand-me-down school uniforms. To supplement the family budget, she did all sorts of jobs, including picking peas in the summer holidays. She gave her earnings to her mother and the farmer let her keep any left-over peas, which she took home and sold to the neighbours. 'They liked fresh peas,' she added.

She was a clever girl who could easily have gone on to university, but girls seldom did in those days, and she left school when she was fifteen to work for the accountants Peat Marwick (now KPMG) in Leeds. She was given the choice of training as a shorthand typist or as a comptometer operator, and wisely she chose the comptometer where the prospects were much greater. Most people today don't know what a comptometer is – or was – but basically it was the first widely used mechanical calculator on which a skilled operator, clever enough to be able to use all her fingers on the keys at the same time, could add up (and subtract) columns of figures fast and accurately. Jean was obviously good at her job because the partners were soon taking her out on audits, working away from home. In those days, company accounts were done manually so a comptometer operator, particularly one as fast as Jean, was a real asset to any team. By the time she was nineteen, she was travelling all over the Midlands on expenses, living away from home all week. At a time when it was very unusual for a young lady to drive let alone own her own car, she bought herself a Morris 1000.

All of this took some time to relate, and we had eaten our dessert by the time she had finished. I asked the waiter for the bill and was ignored. When I asked for it again and there was no sign of it after twenty minutes, I announced, 'I'm not waiting any longer. I'm going.'

I thought I was the cool guy and she'd be impressed with my decisiveness, but in fact she was horrified. 'No, you're not,' she said, 'not without paying the bill.' But I stood up anyway and walked out, expecting her to follow.

I must have waited outside for twenty minutes before, to my huge relief, I heard the 'clip-clop, clip-clop' of her high-heeled shoes behind me. I thought she would be furious with me, but she was more embarrassed than angry. The bill, she said, had still not arrived so she had gone to the bar and paid. Now it was my turn to be embarrassed – not many girls would have picked up the bill on a first date after their host had walked out.

After that we went out regularly, although never back to the Berni Inn. She was the first serious girlfriend I had ever had, and I was her first serious boyfriend, but it was never a normal relationship because of our working lives. Redcar was about ninety minutes' drive from Leeds, and I could never leave the store before it closed on Saturday night at about 6.30 pm and I had to be back at 7 am on Monday morning. That only left Sunday, which we tried to make the most of.

Soon after we met I was moved from Redcar to Boston in Lincolnshire, about 100 miles from Leeds, where she sometimes visited me at the weekends. I took a little flat and was just settling in when I was moved again, first to Birmingham, then to Peterborough, which was a good two-hour drive from Leeds.

I brought Jean home to meet my parents and she remembers my mother looking her up and down before grudgingly offering her a cup of tea – and that was it. My mother could never let herself show any sign of affection, but she must have approved and in her own way I know she liked Jean. It was impossible not to: she was an open, honest and successful girl, with no side to her. My father on the other hand gave her his wholehearted approval, particularly after he spotted her Morris 1000.

In turn I visited her home in Kippax, where the Thorntons lived very different lives to the Adderleys, even eating food different to us: bread dipped in dripping, cod's roe (which is now a delicacy but was common fare in those days) and boiled meats. We were Irish and didn't eat those kinds of things in our household,

Jean's mother suffered from terrible arthritis, so bad that she'd lost her toes because of gangrene and her hands were so swollen she couldn't even dress herself. She could barely walk, and was in constant pain. She had been a sergeant in charge of catering supplies in the war, a fit and energetic lady, but the disease, which had probably been lying dormant for years, suddenly came on when she had her last child at the age of forty. Somehow, for reasons no one could explain, her confinement woke it up, and her immune system went into freefall, affecting her extremities in particular. Her treatment, such as it was, consisted of painkillers and a visit to the wax baths in Harrogate (which did nothing for her). She couldn't hold a knife and fork, and the family legend was that somebody made the mistake of buying her an electric carving knife that she became so good at using that she could get twelve slices out of a currant teacake. She had learned to carve in the army during the war and she had never forgotten.

Whatever her ailments, she was a strict mother. One evening, as I called to take Jean out, she said, 'Make sure you're back by ten!' We arrived back on time but sat in the car outside, just chatting, until, at ten past ten, there was a violent pounding on the roof of my precious Mini. 'Go inside this moment,' Jean's mother shouted, giving the car another whack with her walking stick. When I examined the roof the next day, it was fill of dents.

In February 1969, after we had been going out for more than a year, we began to think about marriage. I had been secretly saving up for an engagement ring and one day I dropped a broad hint that she might look out for something she liked in the local jewellery shops in Leeds. A few weeks later she told me she'd seen a ring she liked in the window of a shop called Zemansky and took me down to see it. It was a beautiful ring, with a sapphire in the middle surrounded by diamonds, the type of thing you'd see Princess Diana wear in later years. Mr Zemansky wanted £65 for it, which was more than I was expecting, and my first reaction was, 'I'm not buying that – it's too expensive.'

Jean went away disappointed and began looking for something less expensive. After she'd gone, I went back to Mr Zemansky, tried to bargain him down, and I bought the ring at a small discount.

The next weekend, I asked her to marry me and her reaction when I produced the ring made it all worthwhile. At that moment I'd have paid Mr Zemansky twice as much just to see her face.

Jean took me home to break the news to her mother and show her the ring. In Jean's house, as in my house, if you wanted permission or approval for anything important, you didn't ask the dad – you asked the mother. So Jean took her into the kitchen, held up her finger and said, 'We're engaged, Mum.'

Instead of saying 'congratulations' or something similar, her mother got up from her chair with astonishing agility and, although she wasn't supposed to be able to walk, she went whizzing into the front room and whizzed back again with one of those jeweller's eyeglasses – I think they call them loupes – and scrutinised the ring in the minutest detail, twisting it this way and that way to catch the light. Because I worked in Woolworths, she was obviously suspicious that I had picked up some bit of rubbish from the jewellery counter. Jean was highly embarrassed, and I began to fear that Mr Zemansky had taken me for a ride. But, having examined it from all angles, her mother finally pronounced the sapphire as genuine – which was the most enthusiastic response we ever got from her.

But she had not finished yet. 'And where are you going to live?' she demanded.

'We eventually hope to have a house of our own,' Jean replied.

'You've always had big ideas!' said her mother witheringly.

Jean and I often thought of that conversation in later life when my business was going well and we lived in a stately home in Stamford, Lincolnshire, with 300 acres of land.

As for the sapphire ring, alas it was stolen in a burglary on our house some years later.

We got married on 20 September 1969, almost two years after we met, when I was twenty-one and Jean was twenty-three. The wedding took place in the Catholic church in Allerton Bywater, near Castleford, and was actually two ceremonies in one. Jean was a Methodist with no intention of converting to Catholicism and I was a (non-practicing) Catholic with no desire to become a Methodist. So a Catholic priest and a Methodist minister jointly presided, which we were told was the first time this had happened. Both reverends took it in their stride, as if it were an everyday event, but it was unusual enough to make the front page of the *Pontefract Express*.

We invited about sixty people to the wedding reception, and I remember it cost 19s 6d per head for a ham sandwich and salad, washed down with a cup of tea. We shared the bill but we still couldn't afford champagne. After we were married, Jean reluctantly quit her job at KPMG and we rented our first house, a pretty little thatched cottage, in Elton, on the outskirts of Peterborough where I was working as a deputy manager. Jean had worked all her adult life for KPMG and was keen to get another job, and one of the big banks, NatWest, offered to take her on and put her through a training course. But before she had even started, she discovered she was pregnant and very correctly wrote to the bank to tell them it would be unfair to ask them to train her and then leave to have the baby. But she got a temporary job working for Hotpoint, a big electrical appliance company, in the accounts department in Peterborough.

On 2 November 1970, fourteen months after we were married, Jean gave birth to our first child, a gorgeous little girl we called Theresa, who became the centre of our lives. I have a picture of me cuddling her as a tiny tot, one of my most precious memories. These were happy days, perhaps the happiest of our lives. I was a young father, with a lovely little child, a good job, a wife I loved, and our own home. Could life get any better?

Fate, however, had something else in store for us. Theresa was less than six months old when Jean put her into her pram and wheeled her out into the garden. When she went to check on her a little later, she wasn't breathing. Only minutes before, she had been laughing and cooing at her mother in the chair, and then she was gone. We never knew the reason why – cot deaths have never been fully explained – but it was the worst blow of our lives, sending me into a deep depression from which it took me a long time to recover. I'm not sure Jean ever did fully recover and both of us still mourn for her. We never did have another daughter, but we did have two sons, Will, born on 4 March 1972, and Jonathan, born on 26 April 1974.

Both boys were to do us proud.

Chapter 7

End of an Era

In retrospect, although I did not see it clearly then, the seeds of Woolworths' decline and eventual demise were already planted well before I moved to the store in West Bromwich, my final posting. Profits began to fall from the late 1960s and went on falling for the next ten years. The first sign of real trouble came in 1968 when Woolworths lost its place as Britain's leading retailer to Marks & Spencer, which passed it in both sales and profits. The management thrashed about, trying everything: an initiative, launched with great fanfare, to stop selling cheap goods and move upmarket, came to nothing; a move into catalogue discount shops, similar to Argos, failed dismally; they tried food-only stores, and when that failed, they tried gardening centres, but that didn't work either.

The senior managers in London were so arrogant, retaining their attitude of 'we're Woolworths, we are the best' although it was clear to everyone – other than themselves – that they were not. They were obsessed by Marks & Spencer and when groups like Asda came on the scene, they dramatically underestimated their threat. The newcomers were hungry, motivated and run by a younger generation of professional managers who owed no allegiance to the traditions of the high street and ran rings around us.

Ironically, the beginning of the end for the great Woolworths store chain, first in America and then Britain, was the launch of the Woolco out-of-town superstores. The American parent opened the prototype in 1962 and, despite mediocre results, continued to expand and imposed the concept on the British company that it still controlled. The first UK Woolco opened in Oadby, Leicester, in 1967, and over the next ten years the group opened another ten even when it was clear they weren't working. Done properly, they could have been the saviour of Woolworths, but old habits die hard and the conservative, dyed-in-the-wool management didn't know how to do it. The British management learned no lessons from the American parent who never got the step-change in performance promised in their business plan and all that happened was their resources drained away. Within a few years all the American Woolco stores were closed and sold as the only way to pay off the mortgages. The British Woolcos followed a couple of years later.

What they should have done was to recruit a hot, young executive from Asda or Tesco and put him in charge, but they didn't think like that. They just thought of jobs for the boys, convinced in their blinkered way they could run everything themselves. There were plenty of young talented managers, myself included, who could have done the job provided we got the right training and directtion. Ironically, the one success they had, after my time, was the acquisition of the B&Q hardware chain which was run by young professionals. But by then it was too late.

Life as a manager of a Woolworts store in Britain became tougher and tougher as the 1970s wore on. To cut costs, in 1971 the group began to convert its shops from conventional behind-the-counter service to a system of centralised payments where goods were paid for and wrapped, theoretically increasing the speed of service and requiring fewer staff. That meant redundancies for the first time in Woolworth's history and a steep fall in morale among the staff, and didn't save a lot of money. Customers, used to the old service, hated it and we lost business.

Everything was against us in the 1970s. On top of the company's internal woes, we had economic recession, strikes, an oil crisis and soaring unemployment. I will never forget the Three-Day Week in February 1974, when the government declared a state of emergency and we only had electric power in the stores on three consecutive days. Worst of all was an inflation rate of 25 per cent, which led to unaffordable wage demands and played havoc with our costs and pricing policy. Around us in the Midlands and North of England, factories were closing, workers were being laid off in their thousands and no one had any money. Woolworths' desperate attempts to modernise came to an abrupt halt in September 1974 when the management in London sent out a message to all managers saying it had been temporarily forced to suspend its investment programme because of the economic crisis and the price controls imposed by the Labour government.

These were tough times to be a store manager, particularly in Britain's industrial heartland, where I was. The old Woolworths, or what was left of it, was changing in front of my eyes and the traditional camaraderie and can-do spirit of the staff was clearly suffering.

Other retailers had the same economic conditions to cope with and most of them came through unscathed. Given half a chance, Woolworths could have done so too. Like many former Woolworths' managers, it almost makes me weep to think of what might have been if we'd had the right people in charge. We had plenty of them in the company, fully capable of turning things around, but they either left or were sacked for not conforming. Three very successful retailers today, Home Bargains, Iceland and my company Dunelm, were started by former Woolworths' managers. Between us we have nearly 2,000 outlets in Britain, many of them old Woolworths' stores, and make profits of more than £1 billion a year. I stayed on until 1978, when I was thirty, increasingly disenchanted with what was going on around me. In the fourteen years I spent at the group, I worked in eleven stores, and every move was a step up for me. If I had stayed on for a few years longer I would almost certainly have made regional manager within a few years – and who knows what beyond that? London seemed a long, long way away but the path I was on inevitably led that way.

But I didn't want to go there any more. The company had clearly lost its way, and it was demoralising watching good managers slip away and our market share and our reputation – and share price – all dropping. Above all, I was fed up with the attitude of the senior management, particularly the buyers, who ruled the roost at head office in Marylebone Road. In my view, the buyers had lost touch with reality, 'captured' by the suppliers who offered them free holidays and cases of champagne at Christmas in return for buying unsuitable products at inflated prices, which we then had to sell at a profit. We all knew they were paying 20p for items they could have got for 10p. That was another lesson I learned in my time as a Woolworths' manager: in Dunelm now, no one is allowed to lunch with a supplier and if a Christmas gift comes in, it goes to the office and is shared out among the staff, whether you're the cleaner or the manager.

Several of the senior Woolworth managers treated store visits like a blood sport, bollocking you as soon as they walked in. A good buyer should have been enthusing the staff about the product he was asking us to sell, but they were doing the opposite. If you contacted head office and complained that some of the products were poor quality or too expensive, you would get a visit and a serious roughing-up. So no one dared – including me. I was a company man who had never known any other working environment, and I didn't question the decisions of the higher-ups. That's how it was and for a time I put up with it.

We were all under huge pressure to hold down costs and keep up profits in our individual stores, and I often did a bit of what we called 'price crowding'. Managers traditionally disguised their shrinkage losses by covertly raising prices on a particular range of goods, using the extra – unrecorded – revenue to fill the gap. For instance, you might sell an item for 12p when the retail price set by the buyers was 10p and put the extra proceeds against your shrinkage elsewhere. It was common practice through the group, and an awful lot of it had been done in Leeds in my early days. Charlie Beck was a master at it, and the management in London knew all about it but let him get away with it because he produced the profits they wanted. He was actually so successful that he was at least partly responsible for introducing the concept of 'overage', which meant generating more money than was lost through shrinkage – a bizarre practice but widely followed by Woolworth managers for years. In fact, it became so deeply embedded that 'shrinkage' became a think of the past, at least on the records (it never went away in reality of course), and if a manager showed shrinkage of more than 2 to 3 per cent he was in trouble with senior management. 'Overages' were seen as the sign of a well-run store, and just so long as the figures looked good, the practice went on.

In the late 1970s, new management was brought in at head office and it didn't take them long to work out there was something strange about the manner in which shrinkage was reported – in fact it wasn't reported at all. The view from London was that 'price crowding' was making us less 'competitive' in a market that was increasingly price sensitive. So the practice was outlawed and, in theory at least, we all went back to declaring profits less shrinkage – which of course meant they were a couple of percentage points lower. The City didn't like that, and the shareholders liked it even less. And the store managers, who made all the group's profits, were caught in the middle of it.

In my case it came to a head when one of the buyers from London, a young chap responsible for electrics, complained that I was selling an electric plug for 33p when the price should have been 30p. When I pointed out that every other manager in the company was doing the same thing to cover shrinkage, he went off the deep end and started shouting at me, saying those days were over and we couldn't get away with it any more. He also complained about one of the displays, which I had personally approved, and we had a right old barney. We didn't quite come to blows but we got close to it. He went back to Marylebone Road and reported me as a troublemaker who was flouting company policy.

The next day I got a call asking me to report immediately to the regional office in Dudley where I was shown into the office of the director, John Dodds, or 'Mr Dodds' as he always was to me – we never used first names at Woolworths, even at manager level. Anyone above you in the management structure was always 'Mister' or 'Sir', even in the late 1970s.

'Adderley,' Mr Dodds began, 'we can't have this sort of behaviour in the company. I've been told to make an example of you. I'm going to have to demote you. We're sending you to Skegness.' Skegness, on the east coast of Lincolnshire, was more than 100 miles from Leicester, two hours' away by car, a long drive home late on a Saturday evening after a six-day working week to see my wife and children. I had moved almost once a year and I'd had enough.

For some time I had been talking to my wife Jean about leaving Woolworths and setting up my own business but I was petrified of leaving the safe haven I knew so well. But Jean was fed up with me banging on about how awful it was and helped make up my mind for me.

'Bill, if you really want to go on your own, this is the opportunity,' she said firmly. 'If you don't leave now, don't ever mention it to me again.' These thoughts flashed through my mind as Mr Dodds looked at me, waiting for me to respond.

I took a deep breath and said firmly, 'I'm not going to Skegness. If you have to move me, find me something closer to home. Otherwise, I'll resign.'

'The order has come from the group CEO personally,' he said, not unsympathetically. 'It's way above my head. You can appeal if you like but you'll have to go down to London to do it.'

The next day I caught the train to King's Cross and went around to the imposing Woolworths' headquarters in Marylebone Road where I was ushered into the office of the CEO.

He didn't take long to get to the point. 'Skegness at £8,000 a year is a good deal,' he said. 'You can take it or leave it.'

'I think I'll leave it,' I said, and got up and left his office – and the company.

I travelled back in the train wondering what I had done and why I had done it. I had no grand plan for what to do next and for the first time in my life I was scared, wondering what the future held for me.

I never dreamed I would find it on a stall in the Leicester market.

Postscript: In September 1981, two years after my departure, a syndicate of institutional investors, led by the City bank Charterhouse Japhet, bought out the American parent and launched a successful £310m takeover bid for Woolworths UK. The new owners changed the group name to Kingfisher and sold off more than 200 unprofitable stores, and tried, with mixed results, to reposition Woolworths as a mid-market retailer. They were no more successful than the old management and increasingly directed their efforts into the more glamorous retail businesses under the same umbrella, the B&Q do-it-yourself chain and Comet, the electrical retailer. The sadly neglected Woolworths retail chain was eventually demerged in 2001 and in 2008, ninety-nine years after the opening of its first store in Britain, it ceased trading.

Of the original 1,000 high street stores, today more than 500 trade under 'value' brands such as Poundland, Poundstretcher, B&M Bargains, and Home Bargains, mostly based on the original Woolworths' variety concept. Iceland, founded by yet another former Woolworths' trainee manager, occupies a further sixty.

To this day, the decline and fall of Woolworths fascinates academics and corporate historians alike, and post-mortems and doctorates are still being written about it. The big question always asked is: why did it fail? In my view, where Woolworths went wrong was in losing sight of its value proposition and its hard-won reputation, dating back to its 'nothing over 6d' origins, for offering the best value at the cheapest prices. It got stuck in what I call 'the mid-market graveyard', offering neither the cheapest nor the best value for money, whereas in my early days – and right up to the early 1970s – it did both.

It was a great story while it lasted. But I guess everything comes to an end.

Chapter 8

Leicester Market

I began my new career on a stall in the Leicester market in January 1979 with a mixture of fear and excitement. I was so used to the rhythm and routine of a big Woolworth store, with its orderliness and camaradie, that at first I missed it hugely. Everything in the market was so different: the people, the hours, the patter, the merchandise, the culture – everything.

But I had burned my bridges and had no other choice than to make a go of it. In my first few days there I observed how the seasoned traders laid out their stalls and greeted their regular customers and the clever ways they made shoppers feel they'd got the bargain of a lifetime. They knew instinctively what would sell and what wouldn't and what price to put on it. Everyone had their own specialty, and I needed mine. The slippers coup had been a one-off and there was no way I could expect another one like it. Eventually I found what I was looking for from an old Woolworths' source. In my last year at the West Brom store, I had some dealings with a guy called Tony Brayshaw who ran the Riverdale Curtains factory in

Leeds, supplying the big store chains, including Woolworths. I had bought some ready-made curtains off him, put them on special sale in Woolworths, and they sold out in a week.

Soon after I opened my stall, I called Tony at his office in Leeds. 'You remember me from Woolworths?' I asked him. 'Well, I've left and I'm on the market now. I'm looking for some curtains – seconds or discontinued lines, something that I can sell on my stall.'

'I have these Woolworths-like imitation velvet curtains, made out of nylon,' he replied a little doubtfully. 'I don't know if they'd be any good for you. I've also got these Marks & Spencer's seconds – would you be interested in those?'

The next day I drove up to Leeds and inspected the merchandise on offer. I didn't much like the Woolworths' imitations but the Marks & Spencer curtains were perfect. They came from Israel, and they were fantastic quality, real value for money. Tony threw in some matching reject M&S bedspreads, we agreed a price and he even offered me credit. 'I know you,' he said, 'and I know you're reputable.' I took everything on offer, including the Woolworths' curtains, and went back to Leicester in my van.

I was just setting out my stall when one of the other stallholders wandered over and asked me what I was selling, and when I said 'curtains', he shook his head sadly. 'You're wasting your time mate. You'll never do any good selling curtains here. Why don't you get into fruit and veg like me?'

His name was Mick Deevy and we formed a friendship which has lasted more than forty years. I still see him and we joke about what might have happened if I'd followed his advice. All I can say is, I'm glad I kept going with curtains. He always brings me a bunch of bananas on my birthday and we have a good laugh.

There was another stallholder nicknamed 'Wolfie', about fifty yards from me, who sold curtains that he bought off the wholesalers and were over-priced for what they were. He had been on the market all his life and his father before him, and had not yet caught up with the fashion for ready-made curtains. Even when it was clear I was taking business away from him, he never showed any hostility to me and sometimes, when he could see I was struggling, he would come over and help me unpack and pack my van. There were others like him. In the Leicester market I never encountered anything other than friendliness.

The M&S curtains were the making of me. I took the label off and I offered them at half-price. They sold so fast I had to keep going back for more and the market superintendent complained that shoppers couldn't get past my stall because of the crowds around it. It was all cash of course, no cheques, which I still kept in a little box under the bed. I spent more than £3,000 of it on a smart second-hand Rover and we took the boys up to Leeds to show my parents and Jean's mother how well I was doing. I felt like King Kong, but my mother-in-law was unimpressed. 'You should have spent the money on a new van,' she remarked as we drove off.

But I didn't mind. Nothing could dent my mood that day.

Initially, I took a stall every week, then twice a week, getting the positions I wanted on Tuesdays and Thursdays. On Fridays we moved to the much-smaller market in Coalville, near where we lived, and on Mondays and Wednesdays I went out buying. I got some real bargains, paying good prices for quality ready-made curtains for which there seemed to be an almost limitless demand from house-proud couples moving into new homes. More by accident than design, I had discovered one of the fastest-growing areas of the furnishings market at just the right time and I was determined to get the most out of it. My experience and my Woolworths contacts gave me a real advantage. My friend Tony Brayshaw was a big help, even keeping me informed about other companies with seconds to sell when he ran out.

Within a few months I had put my Woolworth days behind me and settled into my new life on the market where I was entirely dependent on my own efforts and skills. I loved everything about it: the market, the other stallholders and the thrill of tracking down good merchandise before anyone else did. At Woolworth, you never had to bargain – someone else did the buying for you and prices were set for you at regional or head office level.

Now I had to find my own merchandise and buy it at a price at which I could make a profit. I had never bargained before, but I did now and I found I was good at it – firm but fair. I liked the suppliers, usually small businesses, and they liked me and often kept 'specials' for me which might make all the difference between a good and a bad week.

In those early months on the stall, with the money coming in, I was happier than I had been in all my years at Woolworth. Inadvertently, I had made the right choice.

Chapter 9

Simply Value for Money

From the start of my life on the market, I established two principles that I never wavered from. First, I would never default on a payment. No matter what the financial situation, I always swore that if the whole of the world collapsed and the company owed money, I would pay it out of my own personal funds. I've never left a builder, a plumber or a supplier – anybody – out of pocket. And I've always kept a reserve of cash just in case of a rainy day.

My second principle was that I would never rip people off. Even in those early days, when I was pretty desperate, I always offered value for money. That's how Dunelm traded from the beginning and that's how Dunelm trades today. Value for money is in the genetic structure of the company, the key to its success.

Jean and I shared the work and also the profits, at least notionally. Dunelm was not even a proper company at the beginning: it was a partnership, half-owned by me, half-owned by Jean, and we agreed we would pay ourselves the same – which in the early days was almost nothing. We just thought of making a living, paying the mortgage, putting food on the table and buying clothes for the children. We couldn't afford the fees for private schools for the two boys and, in the early days at least, they went through the state system. We never went on foreign holidays, just grabbed a few days beside the sea when we weren't too busy. We seldom ate out.

Juggling the demands of the business and bringing up two children was not easy, particularly for Jean who bore the brunt of it. It was she who did the books and dealt with the VAT-man, who always haunted her. We never gave the VAT-man a thought in the very early days but once your revenues went above a certain level – I think it was £20,000 a year in those days – you had to register for VAT and submit quarterly accounts. The penalties for being late or providing wrong information were penal and everyone on the market was terrified of the VAT-man who seemed to have it in for small traders.

One of them used to come to our house once a year to check Jean's accounts, a visit we both dreaded, me more than Jean. I dealt in cash only and invoices were either non-existent or just written, often illegibly, on bits of paper torn out of a notebook. The big companies kept proper books but some of the people I dealt with didn't bother and Jean had to work from records that were, to put it mildly, incomplete. But she was meticulous and having worked in a firm of chartered accountants she knew exactly what to do and we never had a problem. Jean still has the original VAT Certificate of Registration, recording Dunelm's registration number as 325 0850 61 and our effective registration date as 1 February 1979, our first official day of trading.

I won't swear that our early VAT returns gave a true and fair account of our actual trading – but they were as close as Jean could make them, which is a lot more than could be said for many of the other traders.

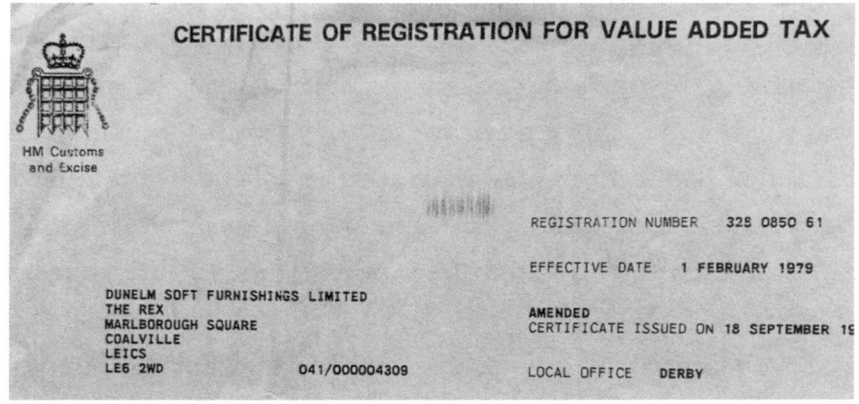

Jean worked with me on the stall in the busy days in the market, mostly manning the till when we were both there, but she was often on her own in the Coalville market on Fridays if I was out buying. The way it worked was that Jean would come to the stall after dropping the children off at school at nine, I would then go out and do some buying, unload my purchases in the garage or warehouse and I'd get back in time for Jean to pick the children up at four.

In those days we never had to worry too much about warehousing space – we sold things as fast as we bought them. Buying the right stuff was even more important than selling it, and it was not always easy. We sold anything I could buy at a good price, moving beyond curtains into duvet covers and bedding and a wider range of what were called in the trade 'soft furnishings'. In the early 1980s, there were still hundreds of textile factories around us in the Northwest and the Midlands, many of them supplying Marks & Spencer or the other big stores groups. Today, almost everything is imported, but the British textile industry, although it was on its last legs, was still limping along when we started. Most of the factories around us had seconds they were keen to sell and if you looked hard enough you could always find a good quality discontinued line caused by a bankruptcy or a change of direction by the retailer.

Seconds, particularly curtains, from Marks & Spencer suppliers were every trader's dream. They sold themselves, like giving away a £10 note for £5. M&S watched over their suppliers like a hawk, setting them incredibly high standards, and if anything was sold as a second with their label still on it, they would cut that supplier off. And if we sold it with the label still on, the suppliers would cut us off too. We never did. Everyone in the market knew what they were simply by the quality and colour.

Someone recently sent me a reference which captured these times. It was from a lady called Yvonne Gregson and says this:

'As a newly married woman in 1980, I went to the market in Leicester and was served by Bill. I was looking for new curtains for my new home. He didn't have my size in the ones of my choice on the stall, but he said he had them in his van and he would run over and get them for me – which he did. The curtains were £3. And that was my encounter with Bill.'

I don't remember her, I'm afraid. But that's the way I built up the business.

Our first VAT return

Sometimes, thinking back, I feel that that some great hidden hand guided my footsteps and led me to the place where I was happy and a career that I was good at. My mother was born on Halloween and my father always said that she was a bit of a psychic, able to see into the future. She was convinced from my earliest years that one day I would be a wealthy man, and she often said so. I'm glad she lived to see it come true.

I've inherited some of her psychic powers and I've seen odd things through my life, maybe two or three a year, many of which have been proved right for reasons I can't explain. I remember being dragged along by some mates to watch England play Australia in a Test match at Trent Bridge. Going in I was stopped by a Sky TV reporter who asked me what I was expecting to see that day. I replied that I didn't know much about cricket, but I expected to see Australia bowled out before lunch. He laughed and moved on to the next person.

Australia won the toss, batted and were all out for sixty, still with some overs left before lunch.

One day I was sitting at my Leicester stall when suddenly I had an odd experience. I'd had a good day, when I'd taken £1,200, and I was getting ready to pack up when I saw this Irish gypsy woman going round the other stallholders offering to read their palm for £10. They mostly told her to clear off but I asked her read mine. I held out my hand and she looked at it for a moment. 'I'm not reading that!' she said, and dashed off. She had been begging the others to let her read their fortunes, but she didn't even wait for the £10 that I was prepared to pay. I was still in shock that evening when I got home to tell Jean. I'm a superstitious person – many Irish people of my generation are – and I found it a deeply disturbing experience. I don't know what she saw, but fifty years later I am still nervously waiting for it to happen.

Chapter 10

Some Hard Lessons

I gained a good reputation on the market as 'Mr Curtains' and I should have been content with that. But I am a restless soul, always looking for something new and in my early days, when I didn't know any better, I made some silly mistakes that I can laugh at now but cost me dearly at the time. Passing a news-wholesaler one day, I had what I thought was a blinding flash of inspiration and went in. 'What happens to all these monthly magazines like *Golfer* or *Yachting Monthly* or *Angling Times* that don't sell? And you get the next month's magazine in?' I asked the lady behind the counter. 'I'll show you,' she replied, readily enough, and took me into the back where there were bundles and bundles of magazines all tied up with string. 'We just dump them,' she said.

'I could take some of them off your hands,' I said boldly.

'Take as many as you like.'

I left with a van load of magazines, all of them out of date, and took them to a car boot sale in a field the following Sunday. I laid them out and put up a sign saying: 'ANY FIVE

SOME HARD LESSONS

for £1.' I sold a few but it was very hard work for not very much reward. It began to rain at lunchtime and my magazines were soon soaked and unsellable. So I drove home, leaving the magazines blowing across the already sodden field. Not one of my proudest moments.

I thought I'd try a different tack a few weeks later when someone offered me a batch of out-of-date cakes that I thought were a sure thing. Nobody wanted to buy them, and, in the end, I just dumped them in a bin. I didn't do any better with a load of pre-worn shoes: there were odd pairs, some with broken heels, others with holes in the soles. I hardly sold any. Another load for the dump. And another lesson learned.

Except I was a slow learner. I had another disaster when I bought a load of quilted nylon bedspreads, 3,000 of them at £2 each. The woman who sold them to me showed me the colours and they were a mixture of cream, which I quite liked, and lime green, which I didn't.

I paid her, put them in the van and took them to the market the next day. That's when I discovered I had been conned, or I had conned myself. Only about ten of them were cream and the others, which I thought were cream, just had a bright cream line across a lime green background. They were really ugly.

That was bad enough but there was worse. When I began laying them out on the stall, I found the frill was only on one side and there was nothing at the back. They must have been made for a hostel or prison with single beds lined up against the wall. Nobody wanted them of course and I had to give them away and dump the rest. Another deal I did wasn't much better. I was in a dry cleaners one day, probably collecting something for Jean, and I looked at the long racks of suits and dresses stretching the length of the shop, wondering idly how anyone could keep track of them. I asked the owner how many people forgot to collect them. 'You'd be surprised,' she said. 'People move, or get sick or even die, and their things sit here for months. We just give them to the charity shop.'

That evening I said to Jean, my sounding board for all my daft ideas, 'Think of it this way: you're a banker in London, you've flown in from America, you're going out to a big dinner, you've got your best suit on, you spill wine down it, take it to the dry cleaners, get a phone call the next day, "Come back to America, we need you." The suit gets left and never claimed. It's all dry-cleaned, and ready to wear. There must be hundreds, thousands, like that across the country.'

The biggest chain of dry cleaners was Sketchley and a few days later I drove over to its office in Leicestershire to see one of the senior managers, and I told him I had a big business selling second-hand goods on the markets around the country. 'I'd like to buy all the clothes that are never collected.'

He agreed to think about it and discuss it with his colleagues. He came back to me a day or two later to say, 'OK, you can have anything you want, 15p a hanger, no matter what's on it: suits, shirts, overcoats, Crombie's, Savile Row, whatever.' He went on to explain that it was all collected from the regions and sent to one centre where it was stored.

'Well, can I pick it up next week?' I asked.

'Yeah, it's all in King's Lynn. I'll tell them to expect you.'

So I drove all the way to King's Lynn and arrived at the Sketchley warehouse where my hopes of another slippers-like coup were quickly dashed. What I hadn't realised, and the guy in Leicester hadn't told me, was that the staff in each branch were allowed first pick and there was nothing left worth buying.

I drove home disconsolately, kicking myself for getting carried away yet again with a crazy scheme. But with each setback I learned something new – mostly not to try it again – and I kept going, more and more determined to make a success of this new career of mine. I was conscious of my change of status in the eyes of Jean's mother and even my own mother who had secretly boasted about her son, the Woolworths' manager. Now, in their eyes, I was a lowly stallholder even if I did have a fancy car. Somehow, I had to turn this into a long-term, profitable and sustainable business, not dependent on crackpot ideas.

People now think it was all easy and my money fell off a tree. Well, it didn't. I went through some bad times and I remember one particular deal that very nearly sunk me. I was offered a big parcel of soft furnishings from a factory – curtains, quilt covers, towels and other assorted goods, all good stuff. They didn't know me at the time and demanded cash up-front on a take-it-or-leave-it basis – either I took the whole parcel or I took nothing. We had just sold the house in Coalville and I had some money in the bank so I took it, leaving myself with barely enough to pay for the petrol. Those goods had to sell fast, but we hit a bad patch in the market and couldn't seem to sell anything. We just about got through but I had some sleepless nights, wondering if I had finally taken one risk too many. There were other deals like that when I was saved only by a few unexpectedly good days in the market, and my dwindling cash under the bed.

My luck turned when I went to see Dorma, one of the best names in the textile industry at that time, to ask for seconds, They started off by telling me they dealt with another guy who took everything they had: curtains, duvets, bedspreads, the lot, all seconds or discontinued lines. But, one of the Dorma people confided, he had become so cocksure of himself that he had started sending stuff back if it didn't sell. 'He's become a real pain in the arse.'

I thought, 'This is my big chance' and jumped in. 'I'll never return anything,' I promised. 'I bury my own dead. You're not going to get anything back from me. And I'll pay you up front.'

The man looked at me closely and I could see him wondering if I was for real. But, after a moment's pause, he said: 'We've got some curtains he's just returned you might like. We made them for Habitat but they sent them back.'

SOME HARD LESSONS

He took me through to the warehouse, and I could see immediately why no one wanted them. They were rubbish, bright red or black with big white polka dots. I looked at them and thought: 'They're awful, but this could be my big opportunity, which may not come again.'

'How much do you want for them?' I asked, and he replied, 'There's 1,500 pairs here and you can have them for two pound a pair.'

They were not worth that, but I just said, 'I'll have them.'

I managed to get rid of them on the market for £2.50 a pair, which didn't even cover my cost, but a week later I went back, found the same man and told him, 'Those curtains you sold me – well, they're gone now. Have you got anything else?' And that blew him away. I wanted to impress him that I could sell anything they gave me, even rubbishy curtains, and I did. He introduced himself as Derek Nott, offered me credit and the other guy got pushed out. I became the sole seller of Dorma's returns, seconds and clearances. Most of the manufacturers, like Derek Nott, treated me with courtesy and genuinely tried to help. They needed to shift old stock almost as much as I needed to buy it, and I became a favoured buyer basically because I always paid my bills within twenty-eight days and never brought anything back.

But not all of them were polite and some of them were downright rude. The rudest of all was John Cotton, a Huddersfield manufacturer of quilts, against whom I held a grudge for years. I called the office one day to make an appointment and was told that the owner, John Cotton, would see me himself at ten o'clock a few days later. Huddersfield is some distance from Leicester, a good two hours by road, so I took the day off, got into my trusty van and drove up. I was there in good time, parked the van and then sat in the reception for an hour and a half before a woman came down from upstairs to say Mr Cotton was very busy. 'He hasn't got time to see you.' No apology, no nothing. Just 'he's too busy to see you'. I was furious.

'Well, I've been sat here for an hour and a half,' I protested angrily. 'I set off at seven this morning to drive here and I've lost an entire day's business on the market where I should be now. I came him up here to buy his quilts and now he won't even talk to me – even though I had an appointment?'

She simply stood her ground, repeating, 'Well, he's busy and he hasn't got time to see you.'

I rarely lost my temper but that time I snapped. 'Tell him this: in years to come, when I'm much bigger, he'll beg to see me. He'll get down on his bended knees to see me. But I'll be too busy to see *him*!' She just smirked and walked away, so I left and drove home, still fuming.

People told me later he was actually a decent and widely respected man and I must have caught him on an off day. But for years I refused to deal with him and it was only after both John Cotton and I had retired that our sons, then running our respective businesses, brought us together. Cotton wanted to make amends. We had lunch and he said he was very sorry, he had been out of order. I don't think he even remembered it and, after twenty-five years, it no longer mattered to me. We shook hands and parted on the best of terms.

I suppose it's the Irish in me that holds on to grudges and it seems utterly pointless now. Today, Cotton's are one of the biggest suppliers of bedding products to Dunelm, running into many millions of pounds. But because of that one slight, they nearly missed out. And so did we!

I had a similar experience with Mike Winch, founder of Candlelight, which is also one of our biggest suppliers today. I was driving my old van down the M1 motorway one day and I saw this sign on a big warehouse near Rotherham saying 'CANDLELIGHT HOMEWARES'. On an impulse, I turned off at the next exit, went back and asked to see the manager. I was expecting a man in a suit but the guy who came out looked like Mick Jagger or one of the Rolling Stones, with long hair and cowboy boots. 'What do you want?' he asked me gruffly, eyeing my old van on his forecourt.

'I've come to buy some clearances off you,' I said, perfectly civilly.

'Well, I haven't got any. Now take that fucking van off my car park and clear off and don't come back,' he almost shouted at me. Unlike John Cotton, I never held Winch's rough greeting against him. He was perfectly within his rights, even if he was a bit rude. I had an appointment with Mr Cotton but I had just turned up at Candlelight without even a phone call. I found a better way of approaching him and we began doing business together. Over the years we became close friends, often doing rock concerts together, which I still enjoy. Candlelight was a relatively small company when we first met, but Mike turned out to be something of a business genius and built a great business. Today, he's a very wealthy man but you'd never know it to look at him – now nearing eighty, he still sports long hair and cowboy boots as he did when I first met him. His story is a remarkable one. He started his career as a fifteen-year-old singer in a rock 'n' roll band, and became a big star, topping the bill at some of the biggest venues in the country. His biggest claim to fame, he always says, is that he played gigs with some of the leading performers of the day, including Cream, Rod Stewart, Ronnie Wood, Pink Floyd and Wilson Pickett. He gave up his singing career in his late twenties to start Candlelight in a barn near Rotherham with a £20 investment. During the miners' strike in 1974, when the lights were going out, he made candles in the kitchen and sold them door-to-door and grew the business from there. He is now one of the biggest suppliers of design-led giftware in the country. Dunelm sells tens of millions of pounds' worth of his merchandise every year. And it all started when I parked my bread van in his car park.

Mike hasn't changed much over the years and is back rocking on with a new band, the Road Runner, which features family members, including his teenage grandchildren. He's a great guy, one of the real characters I've met over the years.

On the whole, Cotton and Candlelight were exceptions and I met with many kindnesses, Dorma being perhaps the most important, where I owe a great deal to Derek Nott, one of my earliest and most important supporters.

Cotton and Candlelight were about the only companies that ever slammed the door in my face. Just two weeks after my rough treatment at Cotton, I went to Fogarty in Boston, who I heard were clearing out quilts and pillows that would sell well on the market. I hadn't made an appointment, but just turned up with Jean and the boys in the van, on the off chance of picking up some seconds. I was told at reception that the man I must see was Mr Head, the sales director, and she would let him know I was waiting for him. He came down a few minutes later, apologising for keeping me waiting. 'Look, I'm very sorry, but I'm busy at the moment,' he said. I said not to worry. 'I just happened to be in the area and dropped in on the spur of the moment.'

I thought Mr Head would go back to his meeting upstairs, but he said. 'Could you wait? I'll be about an hour, but in the meantime, can I get you a coffee? And the children, would they like a soft drink?'

He came back himself a few minutes later with a tray of coffees and KitKats. And I left a couple of hours later with a van full of quilts and pillows.

The contrast between my first experience with Cotton's and Fogarty's could not have been greater. John Cotton treated me badly but then, two weeks later, I found a manager who realised where I was coming from, recognising me as a man just trying to support his family and build up some kind of a business. I've never forgotten Mr Head – and it took me a long time to forgive Mr Cotton.

Life works out in peculiar ways and you can never know what will happen next. I now own Fogarty. And Dorma. We spend millions of pounds each year with Cotton's. And I own 25 per cent of Candlelight.

As they say, what goes around, comes around.

Chapter 11

Dunelm is Born

We still didn't have an official name for our little business until one day in 1980 I was due to take a delivery of a big load of curtains from Dorma, by far and away my biggest purchase yet.

I had developed a very good relationship with Derek Nott who was never too busy to see me even when I was a tiny part of his business. But I was always pushing for more and a few months after that first deal I drove over to the Dorma offices in Bolton and tried to impress Nott and his salesmen, telling them how big I was and how 'I've got this and I've got that' when all I had was a rented market stall a couple of days a week.

I'm sure they could see through the bullshit, but they were nice people and, eventually, after some haggling, they agreed to let me have a big load of sheets, duvet covers and other products. They knew exactly what I was, but they were prepared to take a risk in the belief that one day I might become an important customer (and they were right).

The order was far too big for me to take away in my van, so they agreed to deliver. 'Where's your warehouse?' someone asked. The only warehouse I had was the garage at home, but I couldn't admit that.

'Oh, you can't miss it,' I said airily. 'It's on Greenhill Road, in Coalville. It's the Dunelm Mill Warehouse. The company is called Dunelm Mill Soft Furnishings.' I made it up on the spur of the moment, but I thought the 'Mill' bit gave it a ring of authenticity. Lots of little businesses in Yorkshire and the Northwest were based in old textile mills that had long closed down. And 'soft furnishings' covered just about everything.

'When can you take delivery?' asked the Dorma man and I had to do another quick bit of thinking, The only day I wasn't working in the markets or out buying was Wednesday and I couldn't afford to take another day off, so I said rather grandly, 'Well, I'm fully booked up for deliveries. But I can fit you in on Wednesday next week. Can you get your guy to be there about twelve?'

On Wednesday at twelve, I stood outside on the road watching out for a lorry driver who looked lost and when I spotted him creeping slowly along, peering from side to side, I stopped him and said, 'What are you looking for?'

'I'm looking for the Dunelm Mill Warehouse, which is supposed to be around here. Been driving up and down and can't find it.'

'That's me mate. It's my house here. Look, Dunelm!' and I pointed cheerily at the name on the gate of our house. 'Just drive in and I'll help you put them in the warehouse.' He looked

DUNELM IS BORN

confused because all he could see was the garage, which only took one car and there was no mill in sight.

We unloaded in the driveway, and I took him into the house for a cup of tea, chatted to him nicely, and as he was driving off I almost pleaded with him, 'Do us a favour, mate. When you get back to the factory don't tell them about this.'

He drove off cheerily enough and I never heard another word. But it was a wake-up call, and I registered the name Dunelm Mill Soft Furnishings, with its headquarters in our house in Greenhill Road. I took a little warehouse nearby and put a sign over the door in big letters: 'DUNELM MILL WAREHOUSE.'

And that was how we got our name.

Chapter 12

Saturday Sales

After two years of trading the business was getting onto firmer ground. I still didn't have much in the way of assets: just the old bread van, valued at £280, and my Rover, which was in the books at £3,100. But we had £8,000 in the bank and no overdraft. I was sometimes offered a deal worth two or three times that and I had to take it or lose a supplier. Money in the bank also helped me sleep at night and fortunately I managed to keep my head above water.

But I still didn't have a stall in the Leicester market on Saturdays, by far the busiest day of the week. The regular traders and stallholders hung on to them for dear life. They might be ill or hung-over on other days, but never on a Saturday when every stall on the market was taken. I was trading well on the other days, but the Saturday sales were bigger than the rest of the week put together – and I was not there. The basic price of a Saturday stall on the Leicester market, owned by the council, was £6. But you had to bid for them. I now paid about £25 for the stall that I wanted on Tuesdays and Thursday but Saturday stalls, if they were available at all, went for upwards of £200 which I refused to pay. I was seriously thinking of changing my mind when one day, as I was driving through Loughborough, a market town near Leicester, I saw a sign advertising an antique fair in the town hall for the following Saturday. I stopped the car and went in and asked a helpful lady if the hall was for hire. She said it was, and on the spur of the moment I asked her could I hire it one Saturday later in the month. 'What for?' she asked suspiciously, and I just said: 'Factory sale'.

'Fine,' she replied. 'That'll be £20.'

The town hall was used for council meetings and other events during the week so I couldn't get access until very early Saturday morning a few weeks later. We had to work hard and fast to have everything ready. I spent precious money on posters and ads in the local newspaper, promoting a 'ONE-DAY READY-MADE CURTAIN SALE – DIRECT FROM THE FACTORY', but I had no idea how effective they would be until the doors opened at ten. I needn't have worried – people were already gathering outside, and the large hall was soon full of shoppers eagerly fingering our goods. It was an incredibly busy day and when the doors closed again at three, we had sold almost everything.

I realised I was on to something interesting, and drew up a list of other market towns in an arc around Leicester where I might be able to rent the town halls. It proved astonishingly easy, and I wondered why no one had thought of it before.

Almost all the councils I contacted were delighted to have us and I ended up with a list of twelve town halls, including Wolverhampton, Leeds, Boston, Newark and Huntington; Peterborough even let me borrow the Council Chamber's offices. Each of them was right in the centre of town, perfect for a Saturday sale, all for as little as £20.

I held a sale in each town every three months, which gave me forty-eight sales a year, or almost one a week. I still kept the stall in the Leicester market on Tuesdays and Thursdays and Coalville on Fridays, but the Saturday sales in the town halls became the driving force of the company. Sales-days were hard, gruelling work that left me completely exhausted but it was well worth while. The boys helped and I hired our neighbour's teenage boys, Jonathan Ingleton and Mark and Matthew Graham, to assist with the loading and unloading. I couldn't have managed without them.

Once we began trading in the town halls on Saturdays, I swapped the old bread van for a second-hand Ford Transit, costing all of £1,200, consigning my faithful old van to the scrap-heap. When the business outgrew the new van, I bought a seven-and-a-half ton Mercedes truck, which was driven by either Mark or Jonathan Ingleton while I drove the Ford. We would get our boys out of bed at five in the morning, put them in the back where they instantly went straight back to sleep, drive to the town hall and drag in our merchandise, which then had to be laid out on hastily assembled trestle tables. Jean had to set up her till and I had to be ready at the door at ten to greet people as they arrived and turn on the sales charm as best I could (I discovered I was actually quite good at it). Our ads and posters worked well and there was usually a queue waiting to come in.

The boys, even when they were little, were part of the team. Will helped Jean on the till and his younger brother Jonathan would walk around the sale room, keeping a proprietorial eye on proceedings and making sure people weren't pinching things. At about noon, after what had already been a long day, we'd say to them, 'OK, boys, go get yourself a Coca-Cola and a sandwich.' We'd be in the middle of a big town, surrounded by shoppers, so we thought we could leave them to their own devices, reckoning they couldn't come to much harm. They would go out on their own, walk around the shops and bring something back for their mother and me for lunch.

On one occasion there was a wedding in the church next door and people were chucking confetti and then dropping the boxes on the floor. So the two boys, who were then aged about eight and ten, had this bright idea of scraping up the confetti, putting it back in the boxes, taking it to WH Smith and asking for their money back.

You'd have thought the people in the shop would simply have told them to 'clear off', which is what they used to say to us when we were their age and tried it on. But no, they didn't think like that in WH Smith and called the police. The next thing we knew, two policemen appeared with our little boys who were both in tears. The policemen gave us a good ticking off, and they were right of course – you'd probably get locked up for that now. We were more careful after that.

Within a year, our Saturday sales had become a fixture in the towns, and we were often told by the locals that they saved up to buy from us. As time went on, I was able to source more goods, and the sales became bigger and more profitable.

The suppliers were very loyal to me, and they often kept things back that they thought I might like. On one occasion, Fogarty offered me a van load of rugs, which I bought, and then noticed a large stack of sheets at the back of the warehouse. 'What about those?' I asked the sales person. 'There's about two and half thousand there,' she said. 'You can have them for a penny – the lot!' I sold them for £2.99 each.

Fogarty were often good to me. They sponsored an annual event for a Dr Barnardo's Sports Day, and one year they built a mountain of pillows about 40-foot high in a field near London, all blue with a white top so it looked like a snow-covered mountain. The pillows were just there for the children to jump on and the Fogarty guy didn't know what to do with them afterwards. He rang me the next day and said, 'Bill, there's 4,000 pillows in a field if you want them – you can have them for nothing if you just take them away.' There were three van loads of them and I sold them for 99p each.

People ask me how I sold so many pillows and curtains on a small stall in the market. The answer was that I would put out

Jean and I, dressed for dinner at our local golf club.

An evening out in the pub, with my great pal, Keith McIver, and his wife, Barbara.

Below: Jean, like me, took up golf in her forties and became an accomplished player. Here she is with two of her many trophies. Below right: with Keith McIver, a Dunelm supplier who became my best friend after our first deal.

Below: me (right), with my brother Peter (far left), my son Will and my nephew Oliver.

The Adderley family: Jonathan, our youngest son, is on the left and Will is on the right.

Above: at Will's wedding to Nadine Rose, in 2001.

Jean and me with five of our (six) grandchildren. Ava, with a cake she baked for my birthday. Left: Fred (back row) and Ced (front left), Will's two sons. Right of Ava are George and Charlie, Jonathan's boys.

Jean's siblings: from the left, Janet, Ken, Joan and Jean.

Will gets his knighthood for services to charity from Princess Anne at Windsor Castle. Right: the newly ennobled Sir Will and Lady Adderley.

Below: Will and Nadine with their lovely family, Fred, on the left, Ced and Ava.

My youngest son Jonathan with his former partner Jennie and their son George. Below: a few days before Christmas 2022, there was a knock on the door and when I opened it Jonathan said, 'I've got a surprise for you, Dad.' He then presented me this gorgeous little girl, Eve, grandchild number six!

Bottom left: baby Eve, and right, my goddaughter Grace.

These are my favourite photographs: my granddaughter Ava as a baby (top) and as a beautiful young lady. She was my favourite until Eve came along. Now I've got two favourites.

The *Leicester Mercury* did an interview with me and took this picture. Below: the coast of Donegal, near Clonmany, where I spent many happy days as a boy. It was the poorest corner of Ireland in those days, but in 2017 it claimed the top spot on *National Geographic Traveller's* 'Cool List' of destinations. I still have nineteen cousins there.

Photo: *Shutterstock*

as many as I could and leave the rest in the van. Every time I sold out, I would say to the woman next to me, 'Just watch the stall for a minute please,' run to the van and bring back another double armful. It was hard work, but I never minded that. I was tough and fit and felt I could tackle anything.

I sold some very odd merchandise in my days on the market. Tony Brayshaw, my friend from Riverdale Curtains in Leeds who had started me off in the first place, called me one day to say he had 7,000 pairs of polyester curtains that Woolworths had ordered and then cancelled. 'They're called Figaro, after the opera I suppose, and they're really fancy, all swirls and swags. I don't think you'll like them,' he warned. 'But they're choking up the warehouse and you can have them – any size – for a pound a pair. As long as you take the lot.'

I didn't know anything about opera, so Figaro meant nothing to me, but I did know about curtains, and these were really dreadful. They came in either blue-and-white or brown-and-white, in shapes and colours that some mad designer must have come up with before he got sacked. I wasn't surprised that Woolworths rejected them and I couldn't imagine anyone putting them up in their living rooms. But I took them anyway and set them out on the stall as attractively as I could with a notice: 'Any size £2.99'.

At first, they barely sold at all and then, for no reason that I could see, sales began to pick up and people came to the stall specifically asking for 'them Figaro curtains'. It was only when

Jean and I were driving along the Melton Road in Leicester one day that we discovered why: there was a large block of flats where every window had a pair of Figaro curtains. They were obviously high fashion in Melton Road and later on in other blocks in the area.

And that's how the business developed. I had no master plan and never thought ahead more than a few weeks at a time. Opportunities just came along, and I seized them. In our second full year, 1980, we doubled turnover to £91,000 and profits from £6,000 to £12,000, a fortune by our standards. Only the very top managers at Woolworths were earning that at the time, and every day that passed I thanked my lucky stars for the way things had worked out.

I bought £76,000 worth of goods that year and had to move to a bigger warehouse. I never asked for credit and paid for everything up front in cash, which the suppliers loved me for. No one else did that. The next year, 1981, our third in business, was by far and away our best yet. Sales were now averaging £3,000 a week and we sometimes had days when we took more than £10,000; our best day ever was £16,000 in five hours. You could buy two houses for that then.

The Adderley family's share of profits that year – just Jean and me – was more than £12,000 each.

Even when we were doing well, we kept on the Friday stall on the market in Coalville, although it was barely worth our while financially. Jean liked it as it was only a few minutes' drive from the boys' school, and she loved to meet and chat with the local people who often came to the stall just for a chat. Coalville, as the name implies, was built around – actually on top of – the coal mines that had once made it a prosperous, thriving town. But it was now dying, killed off by the miners' strikes in the 1970s and confrontation with the Thatcher government that basically destroyed the coal industry. In 1980, when we opened our stall, the last of the mines was closing and half the town seemed to be unemployed or living on benefits. (I'm told there are no working coal mines in Britain today). Money was short, which made the market in Marlborough Square more attractive than the big supermarket groups that had opened on the edge of town.

Every week an old miner would come round the market selling sweepstake tickets to raise money for the miners' welfare fund. Jean always bought at least one but never expected to win. You picked two numbers from 0 to 99 and there would be a prize each week for the person who guessed right – and got them in the correct order. One day, just before Christmas, Jean came home from the market in floods of tears. 'Why are you crying?' I asked her, thinking there had been a family death or something had happened to one of the boys.

'I won the miners' sweep!' she said and burst into tears again.

'So what are you crying for?' I asked in growing bewilderment.

There had been no winner for four weeks so the prize was about £500, a lot of money if you were a poor miner's wife.

'A few years ago, when we were really struggling,' Jean sobbed, '£500 would have made all the difference between us getting through Christmas with presents and things, or going without. But I just put it in my pocket and went on selling things on the stall as if it were nothing.'

In the end I think she gave it away and someone had a good Christmas.

I was continually looking for new ranges and kept adding. I bought a big shipment of cups and saucers, which sold well. I went on into ornaments, pots and pans, artificial flowers, anything that came under the rough description of homeware.

I had my own individual way of doing business, which was straightforward and upfront, and the suppliers appreciated it. Once I had agreed to take something, I stuck to my promise never to return it and, if I couldn't sell it, I either gave it away or dumped it. I took a profit on the stalls but never an exorbitant one and shoppers got to know that. Reputations mattered in the market, as they do everywhere in life.

That's how I did business then, and that's how I continued to do business even when sales were in the hundreds of millions. The same principles apply, whether you're big or small, rich or poor. I've stuck to them all my life.

Chapter 13

Churchgate

By 1983 the business was really humming. Sales that year increased from £214,000 to £478,000 and profits doubled to £64,000, split 50–50 between Jean and me. Profits doubled again in 1984, and by 1985 they topped £200,000, or £4,000 a week. The more we grew, the harder I worked – if that was possible. I got up before dawn and arrived home late in the evening, including weekends. It really was 24/7, without even Sundays off.

I needed more selling space where I could offer a wider range of merchandise and I couldn't do it on a market stall three days a week, and one townhall sale on Saturdays. We were now doing so well that we couldn't get enough seconds and were selling items bought direct from the manufacturer or wholesaler. We were even designing our own merchandise and putting them on the makeshift shelves on the stalls, which was never very satisfactory.

The biggest problem with a market stall – or a Saturday sale – was that the only time you sold anything was when you were physically there. If you decided to take a day off – and I very seldom did – you took nothing. I had now been doing it for five years, working all hours humping heavy weights in and out of the vans, setting up trestle tables with new displays and then taking it all down again at the close of the day. It was time to move on. I would open a shop.

Early in 1984 I acquired an old iron foundry – they had been metal-platers, working with very toxic acids – on a street corner on Churchgate, right in the centre of Leicester. The top floor was occupied by a printer and on the next floor down there was a guy making jeans. I kept the ground floor and the first floor and let out the rest.

Initially, I rented the building but when the owner offered it to me, I bought it for £35,000 and set to work immediately to convert it into a shop. I had a stroke of good fortune when I saw some men removing fixtures from a closing-down Co-op in Oadby. I stopped the car and asked them where they were taking them and one of them grunted, 'Storage.'

I said, 'I'll give you 200 quid for the lot.' They just handed me the key to the Co-op and drove off, probably to the nearest pub.

I took everything to Churchgate, fitting out my first store at a fraction of the cost I had budgeted for.

I was very proud of that store (it's the cover of this book). I painted the front green and white, the colours that would become the emblem of the Dunelm company. I wanted it to look as much like a factory shop as possible and put a large 'DUNELM MILL' sign on the front, which would remain the name we traded under until we went public some years later.

The inside of the shop, when we finally opened, was pretty basic, but it allowed me to display a wider range of merchandise, including ornaments, pots and pans, artificial flowers and a big range of crockery. Without realising it, I had created the first specialist homeware store in Britain, the first in a chain of them.Before it was even open I bought a site for another store, the old Rex Cinema in Coalville, which I got for £52,000. It still had its cinema seats – 1,200 of them – so I got a local guy to help me take them out and we levelled the floor all the way to the screen. While we were working on it, we had people coming in to ask if they could buy a particular seat, which puzzled me at first. The cinema, like many at the time, had originally installed double seats at the back where courting couples could get up to whatever they got up to. One day a middle-aged man came in and asked to buy seat 10 to 12, a double seat in the back row. 'That's where my son was conceived,' he explained. 'I'd like it as a keepsake.' We sold a few more like that and stored the rest of the seats in the space under the new floor and for all I know they're still there.

We left the old Rex Cinema sign above the door underneath the more prominent Dunelm Mill sign and it became Shop Number 2. It also became the new registered office of the company, which served us well until Dunelm moved to larger premises some years later. I'm told the old shop is derelict now, like so many of the old town centres in England.

★★★★★

I didn't realise it at the time, but in moving from market stall to shops I was following in the footsteps of some of the most illustrious British retailers of all time. Michael Marks, the founder of Marks & Spencer, started off as a pedlar selling cotton reels, buttons, soap and candles door-to-door in the villages around Leeds, including Castleford where Jean went to school. A Jewish immigrant from Russia who arrived in England in 1882, he didn't speak any English, so he attached a sign to his display tray, which he hung around his neck, which read, 'Don't ask the price – it's a penny'. He soon graduated to a stall in the Kirkgate open-air market in Leeds, operating off a trestle table two days a week, still selling everything for a penny. Someone said of him, 'To be a successful stallholder he must have had some charm' and people have said the same about me, although I was never conscious of it. I was just me, no airs and no graces – but maybe just a little charm, too? Within a few years, Marks grew his business to twelve stalls. My maximum was two, one in Leicester two days a week and one in Coalville on Fridays. But my big earner was my Saturday sales in the town halls, which I had all to myself and was much bigger than any stall. Marks lived in a small terrace house in Trafalgar Street on the north side of Leeds, about six miles from Middleton where I was brought up. Leeds had some rough areas in my time, but it was said to be even rougher in Marks's day, 'a hotbed of drunkenness and immorality, the haunt of criminals' as one historian called it, with not a little exaggeration. He later moved to Wigan, which had a thriving Jewish community, and finally to Manchester where he built his first head office in Derby Street.

As a matter of interest, I often wondered who the 'Spencer' was in the partnership of Marks & Spencer and was inspired to do a bit of research. Thomas Spencer was the senior cashier of a Leeds-based wholesaler called Dewhirst, a gentile who in 1894 invested his life savings of £300 to buy a half-share in Marks's penny bazaar business. Spencer lasted nine years in the business before retiring to the life of a country gentleman, living off his half-share of the burgeoning profits generated by his hard-working partner. He died, aged fifty-three, apparently from drink 'and a life of ease'. Within a few months Marks was also dead, the result of 'a frail constitution, overwork and cheap cigars', according to one of his biographers. He was only forty-seven. His daughter Rebecca married the young Israel Sieff and for the next century Marks & Spencer was run by the Marks and Sieff families, which is how I remember it.

There was another iconic retailing figure equally relevant to my humble beginnings. Jack Cohen, founder of Tesco, started with a market stall in Hackney, London's East End, and opened his first shop a few years later; it had no doors or windows and looked as much like a market stall as he could make it, just as Marks's penny bazaars did. Some of Tesco's stores today are vast: the Slough branch is 185,000 sq ft, which is nearly four acres. (Dunelm's biggest is just over 30,000).

★★★★★

Within a year of opening, the two Dunelm shops, small though they were, had taken over as the driving force behind my little business. In the year ended 30 June 1988, as Coalville kicked in, turnover hit £3.6 million, doubling in three years, and it kept growing. Dunelm was rapidly developing into a sizeable retail business, and we now employed forty-two people, four, including Jean, in the office and the others in the stores. The wage bill by then was more than £200,000 and rising.

Jean and I could now call ourselves millionaires, although our lifestyles didn't change much – we were too busy for that. Dunelm only had two shareholders, Jean and me. And it only had two directors: Jean and me. There was no finance director. There was not even a company secretary. Jean did all that, coping brilliantly with the books until it became too big for her and we had to employ a firm of professional accountants to prepare the accounts. Jean, however, insisted on remaining involved right up to the time we floated on the stock market in 2006 when she finally stepped down as company secretary.

I did everything else: buying, selling, marketing (we had an advertising budget of £20,000, which we mostly spent in local newspapers), van driving and general dogsbody, loading and unloading until my shoulders ached. Ten years after we started, we were generating cash at a rate of more than £400,000 a year, but we paid no dividends and Jean and I took a modest salary of £25,000 a year each – everything else went back into the company.

In 1989 revenues topped £4.5 million and profits were nearly £500,000, or £10,000 a week – a long, long way from our first year when we thought ourselves very fortunate to make a profit at all. We were a private company, which meant we didn't have to publish our accounts and other than our auditors and finance staff, no one had a clue what profit we were making. We didn't lead an ostentatious life, and we remained plain 'Bill and Jean' to our neighbours and friends, with no airs and no social pretensions.

But once I opened my first shop, the vision that had been forming in my mind since that first day in the market became a lot clearer. I had believed from the beginning that I could build a big business and now I could see the way to achieving it. The shops turned Dunelm into what I would call a 'proper retail company' rather than a business living day-to-day on the market, dependent on whether we turned up or not. Now I could hire people to run the shops and leave them to it (although I didn't of course – I visited every day).

The Rex Cinema gave us a base for expansion with warehousing space that we badly needed. Every time I thought we had ample warehousing space, the business out-grew it. By 1989 we had stock worth nearly £500,000 in our warehouses, an inconceivable amount compared to the days when we used to keep it in the garage at Dunelm, our house in Coalville. Half a million pounds' worth is an awful lot of curtains, quilts, pillows and other soft furnishings and took a large amount of space. The suppliers now offered us credit and I no longer had to fetch it in the van – they delivered direct to the warehouse.

On my travels up and down the country, I always stopped off at the local shopping centres or city centres to study what was happening there, all the time learning and seeing where I could improve my little business. I learned a lot about homeware by studying John Lewis, the icon of the sector, but I knew I could never afford their fancy premises on prime sites. Queensway Discount Warehouses was a better model. It was started by a man called Gerry Parish who in the late 1960s rented a disused warehouse near Norwich and with just £50 set up Britain's first out-of-town discount store, initially selling just carpets.

In 1978, while I was still working for Woolworths, Phil Harris bought them for £2 million, changed the name to Harris Queensway and did a wonderful job converting them into stores that still looked like warehouses on the outside but inside they were divided into 'room-sets' to show bedrooms, dining rooms and kitchens just as they might look at home. It was a brilliant formula and drove the profits of Harris Queensway into the stratosphere.

I admired Phil, one of the great retailers of my lifetime, and learned a lot just by seeing how he laid out his stores and promoted his sales. By the time I began seriously looking at out-of-town shops, purpose-built shopping centres with plenty of car-parking space were all the fashion. All the big chains were there, each with their own specialities: B&Q sold DIY products, Comet sold electrical goods (both had been part of Woolworths), Halfords sold car parts and Harris Queensway sold carpets and furniture. No one specialised in homeware, for which, I was convinced, there was a big market.

By the early 1990s, we had eighteen shops, and we were again running out of space. That's when I made our first serious acquisition. For some years I had been buying bits and bobs off Peter Haycock, a wholesaler who had an out-of-town warehouse near Rotherham, just off the M1. I heard he was struggling and approached him to see if he was prepared to sell it to me. He indicated he was but he wanted £1 million for it, which I thought was far more than it was worth.

But I agreed to go up and see him and took my eldest son Will along with me. He was at Nottingham University and I wanted him to gain some experience of deal-making if he came to work full-time for us – which I hoped he would.

Peter Haycock's business consisted of a large rented building that was really not much more than a shed, with a huge car park on which you could have built fifty houses. It was in a small shopping centre – just three units – on the edge of town where the rental was cheap. The building itself had a short-term lease and was basically worth nothing, so essentially I would be buying the stock – most of which I didn't want.

Haycock sold just about everything, from jeans and shoes to sweets and food, a huge range that seemed senseless to me. I didn't want anything other than the homeware, which was confined to a distant corner of the premises. The rest of the stock would be sold for whatever I could get.

There was a café where Will and I crept in quietly, without announcing ourselves, and ordered a cup of tea. It was a terrible hole, a stopover for truck-drivers who pulled into the car park, air brakes hissing, and I could see they were regulars by the way they greeted the staff and ordered their eggs and chips. The café – if you could call it that – was run by a lady called Maureen who was, to my eye, greatly over-generous with the portions. 'I've given you a lot more chips, Harry,' she would say, adding another portion without charging for it. I had never seen so many chips in my life. The café, I decided there and then, would be the first thing to go, closely followed by Maureen. Lorry drivers were not the clientele I wanted. I would replace it with the kind of coffee bar we had at the bigger Woolworths' stores, a destination in its own right where customers could take a break between purchases.

I ended up offering Haycock £330,000 for the entire business, which was about the value of his stock, and after some negotiation he accepted. But when our two sets of lawyers sat down to complete the deal, we discovered a snag that virtually killed it. Peter had installed a fancy computerised till system, unusual in those days, and wanted us to take over the lease on it. My attitude to computers was that I didn't understand them, didn't much like them, but knew that as my business grew and became more complex I would need them one day. But I was in no hurry – I had long decided to let other retailers spend their money developing them and, when they got them right and ironed out the bugs, I would think seriously about them. I was certainly not going to be bounced into taking on the expensive lease for an over-elaborate system I didn't need.

Will and I stepped outside the meeting for a chat, and when we went back in, I said we would go ahead with the deal – but without the computer system which Peter could do what he liked with as long as he removed it. Eventually, after a lot of argument, he gave in, and we got the business for the value of the stock.

As soon as we completed the deal, I drove up to Rotherham and got the staff together. They were clearly nervous, fearing the worst, knowing that good jobs were scarce in the area. So

I opened with some reassurance. 'I want you all to stay,' I told them, and I could almost hear the sighs of relief. 'But things from now on will be different,' I went on. 'We are no longer going to be selling all this stuff,' I said, gesturing at the counters and floor piled high with every conceivable item. 'We will sell it all off and close the café, which is just a cheap stop-over for lorry drivers. We're going to concentrate completely on soft furnishings from now on.'

Some of the girls burst out laughing at that. How would I fill the space with just homeware, someone asked me. And who would come to a small out-of-town shopping centre near Rotherham to buy it?

'You'll see,' was all I said.

I advertised a huge clearance sale and within a week almost everything had gone. I packed up all that was left and gave it to a charity shop and set about replacing it with the widest range of goods I had ever sold.

I had a good idea of what we would fill the store with, which was just about everything for the home, from cups and saucers, vases, curtains, towels, lighting, glassware, bathroom mats, bed linen, rugs and small furniture, anything people could take away in their cars. I knew exactly what I wanted the shop to look like and I spent a lot of time and effort improving the look of the building and getting the display just right, setting the goods out attractively so that anything we put into this environment would sell – which it did.

I was determined there would always be a special offer in the store, creating an extra degree of excitement and making shoppers feel they were getting a real bargain – which in truth they were. My days on the market had given me contacts everywhere and I was able to source seconds or clearances that sold out in days. When I ran out of local sources, I went to the big distributors and negotiated a deal on goods made in the Far East. There would of course be only a limited amount of 'special' stock available but that was all the better – shoppers would know they had to get in quick or lose out. And I wanted people to be able to have a good feel before they bought: for instance, one duvet would always be out of its cover beside a stack of duvets (very big sellers) for people to touch. Shoppers liked that.

The store was a success from the moment we opened the doors, exceeding even my high expectations. In our first full year our takings were more than £1 million, ten times what we were taking in the average high street store. I never opened another high street store.

I'm happy to say that some of the girls who openly scoffed at me when I bought the Rotherham store are still working for Dunelm today, more than thirty years later.

And that was it. In 1992 the group's turnover, powered by the new store, rose by more than £3 million to £7.8 million. We were up and running on out-of-town stores.

Chapter 14

Golf

It was only after we opened our second superstore in 1992 that I finally gave up the stall in Leicester market and stopped the Saturday sales in town halls. I was forty-four and had been managing my own stall since I left Woolworths at the age of thirty. I didn't need the money any more – that year we made a profit of nearly £2 million – and to be frank I had kept up the stall in the last few years largely because I enjoyed it and knew I would miss it. But it was time to move on.

People today have no idea what an old-style traditional market was like, particularly Leicester market, which was arguably the best market – it was certainly the biggest – in Britain. There was a real buzz about it, a wonderful feeling of camaraderie and fellowship among the regular stallholders, many of whom had been there for more than thirty years, and some even longer. It was like going to the club (a working man's club of course), swapping stories and gossip, discussing our respective trading, catching up on family news. You could get just about everything in the market at a better price than the big stores offered, and quite a few housewives came every day to buy their fruit and veg, meat and fish. Many of the stallholders, like me, specialised in seconds or clearances and if I had a new line of M&S curtains or something else that was good, they were pleased for me, and I felt the same about them. If I needed someone to keep an eye on my stall, I would simply ask the stallholder next door. Anyone could take a stall on the market simply by paying the Toby, so there were no barriers to entry, and everyone was equal. As time went on, however, many of the old-timers retired and the new generation wasn't interested in the hard work involved. Others couldn't hack it because they didn't know how to source merchandise as cheaply as we regulars did, and others left when they had made enough money to start their own shops. There were more glamorous jobs on offer in the big store companies, which were expanding fast and always on the lookout for good retailers.

Quitting the market left me with time on my hands for the first time in my life, a strange feeling that at first I couldn't get used to. So I took up golf.

It came about like this. One of our suppliers was a wonderful family-run business, J C McIver, which manufactued ready-made curtains for the big mail order companies such as Grattan, Freemans and GUS. I regularly bought seconds off them when I was still on the market and usually visited their showroom when I was doing my buying rounds in the North. I had got to know the founder, Keith McIver, a real entrepreneur who, in the early 1980s, had set up a factory near Manchester where he employed 60 machinists. His velvet curtains were all stamped 'Made in the UK' which appealed to me – wherever I could, I always bought goods made in Britain, although as time went on that became more difficult.

I was mainly interested in his curtains, which were very high quality, but one day he showed me a line in tablecloths that were marked for Freemans at £2.99. It didn't take me more than a glance to see they were cheap polyester rubbish. 'I need to get rid of them,' he said.

'Well, I'm not taking them,' I replied firmly.

'You can have them for half price,' he said temptingly.

I could see he was eager for a deal, so, after thinking about it for a moment, I said, 'I'll tell you what I'll do. I'll give you 75p for them and I'll try to sell them at one pound fifty.'

'But they're marked £2.99,' he protested. 'What about half price?'

When I still said No, he dropped his price to £1.20. 'That's my final offer.'

I still wasn't interested and let the matter drop, thinking that was that.

But he called me the next morning and said, 'Where do you want these tablecloths delivered?'

I couldn't believe this. 'I told you I didn't want them!' I replied. 'I'd have them at 75p, but you want £1.20 for them, so there's no deal.'

'No, no, no, no,' he said. 'You said you'd have them at £1.20.'

'No, I said 75p!'

This went on for some time until, realising I meant it, he suddenly said, 'I'll tell you what I'll do. I'll toss you for it.' That dumbfounded me. How would that work? He was in Manchester, I was in Leicester, and I couldn't see the coin. But I wanted to look like I was big enough to handle this stuff – one of the lads if you like, although I was new to this particular game.

'OK. Go on then.'

There was a pause, and then he came back on the line to say, 'Damn it! I've lost.'

I don't know to this day whether that was a double bluff, or his way of getting me to trust him. He delivered the tablecloths, I paid him 75p for them and I managed to sell them for £1.50. Whatever his game was, it worked because after that I would have trusted him with my life. He became a dear friend, one of my closest buddies.

Once a month he would send his general manager, a man called John Shaw, to my house and we would tally up what I owed, and settle. Usually, this process would take no more than a few hours but if it took longer he would stay over and take Jean and me out for a slap-up dinner, paying with the cash I had given him earlier in the day. Two or three bottles of good wine made a considerable dent in it and I can't imagine how he reconciled the books back at head office.

John was an ex-pro golfer and, one day, when we had settled our business by ten o'clock in the morning, he said, 'Let's have a game of golf. I've got a golf bag in the car. Where's the nearest golf club?'

As it happened, there was one just down the road and he insisted on taking me there. When I protested that I didn't play golf, he just said cheerily, 'I'll show you. I used to do this for a living.' I didn't have any clubs but he said we'd hire them. 'I'll talk to the pro.'

The pro fitted me out with a bag of clubs, and we went out on to the driving range where he showed me how to hold the club and practice my swing and soon I was driving a respectable distance, more or less in the right direction. I had got the bug, which has lasted a lifetime.

Golf is a great way of making friends and, after the tablecloth episode, I regularly played with Keith, or one of the other suppliers who loved their game of golf and were very happy to play in mid-week with a customer.

To this day many of my best friends are golfers I met back in the days when I was doing the rounds, and some years ago we formed a group we grandly call the Ravensbourne Society, which goes away for a golfing weekend twice a year. Our trip to Blackpool is X-rated and not for a family book like this but, on the whole we behave reasonably well, if a little raucously at times.

If I played golf on a Saturday morning, I would stop by one of the stores in the afternoon just to see what was going on. I never told the manager I was coming, although I always announced myself when I arrived rather than have them find me snooping around their store. One Saturday I walked into the Derby store at about one o'clock still dressed in my golf clothes and made my way to the customer services point. It was manned by a student, as it often was on a Saturday, and I said politely to her, 'Hello. Could you tell me who's in charge today?'

'It's Sandra,' she said, clearly puzzled. The poor girl had only been with us for a few weeks and clearly had no idea who I was.

'Could you get her on the intercom for me?' I asked.

'Who shall I say wants her?'

'Tell her it's Bill, the chairman.' She eyed me up and down suspiciously for a moment.

'Are you Bill? Funny. I'd heard you were a lot scruffier than that!'

I roared with laughter and have dined off the story ever since. I had grown up in Woolworths where seniority was everything and you called people above you in the pecking order 'Sir'. The culture I set out to create at Dunelm was the opposite. I liked it informal and friendly, with nobody pulling rank and no special privilege for anyone, including me. We had no special staff canteen, as we had at Woolworths, no special parking, and no 'Sirs' or 'Madams'. I was just plain Bill and was happy to be called that even by a young student.

That little girl that day proved I had succeeded. Whatever happened at head office, down here on the shop floor 'Bill' was the man.

Eventually I got my golf handicap down to five, not bad for a man who didn't take it up until he was in his mid-forties, and I still get a lot of fun out of it. So does Jean, who took it up at the same time, and has become a more than adequate player – although, for the sake of our relationship, we seldom play together.

Chapter 15

The Dunelm Model

Rotherham established the format, and after that I looked only for out-of-town sites that could house a superstore with 25,000 sq ft to 30,000 sq ft of selling space plus an adequate car park. We still had more than twenty high street shops and they were profitable, but as the leases ran out, we didn't renew them. But it was not always easy to find a good out-of-town site that fitted the tight criteria we set. I refused to pay the rentals accepted by other groups, such as Carpetright (Philip Harris's new company after Harris Queensway was taken over), JD Sports, B&Q or Currys, and we must have turned down hundreds of sites. I always drove a hard bargain, insisting on fifteen-year leases with five-year reviews and a cap on increases.

We were not looking for prime sites in new developments where M&S or one of the other big stores was the anchor, and rentals were very high (except for M&S, which always got a good deal). I was prepared to accept less attractive, sometimes 'solus', sites where Dunelm Mill would have to rely on its wide range of homeware and clever advertising to attract new customers. We didn't do carpets, a market dominated by Carpetright, and we didn't do kitchen tables, but we carried every kind of homeware for the kitchen, the bedroom, the bathroom and even rugs and small furniture for the living room. In the early days we didn't do couches or beds either but, later, when we could deliver, we did. We sold pillows (forty different kinds of them at prices ranging from £2.99 to £49.99) and thousands of duvets and quilts. The modern-day Dunelm store offers more than 100,000 different items but we started off with only a few thousand and expanded rapidly.

We always had a sale going on, another way of attracting customers to a new shop. It was also profitable and 'special' buys usually accounted for 20 per cent of turnover. It all fitted into the slogan we used from the start – 'Simply Value for Money' – which was clearly visible in all the stores, as indeed was the in-store strapline: 'DEPARTMENT STORE QUALITY AT HALF THE PRICE'. To make sure we met that target, I toured the department stores, particularly John Lewis, which had a big store in Leicester, all the time comparing prices and service.

A point of difference I insisted on was a custom-made curtain facility in the stores, which proved very popular and was another reason for people coming into the shop. When we couldn't find anyone to make them for us, we made them ourselves.

All this makes the stores sound like warehouses with goods piled up in unsightly heaps against the wall. In fact, they were the opposite. I wanted the new stores to offer an attractive and welcoming environment with customers encouraged to browse in a visually impressive, exciting and well-stocked space. Good service was vital, and we put a lot of effort into training the staff to be cheerful, focused, helpful and friendly, differentiating us from the supermarkets that offered ranges of homeware at low prices but nothing in the way of assisted selling. I took personal responsibility for staff relations, which I have always been good at it.

Both our boys joined Dunelm, Will to stay for the long-term, Jonathan for about five years. They had spent a large part of their childhood and teenage years helping us on the stalls and the Saturday sales, and I don't know what we'd have done without them. They missed out on a lot of school activities, including sports and playing with their friends. But I don't remember either of them complaining, even when we dragged them out of bed at five in the morning to set off for the Saturday sales.

The two boys were very different, and I sometimes wondered if they had grown up in the same household. Will was always more enthusiastic than his brother who was more laid back and lacked Will's driving ambition. Jonathan left school at sixteen, as I did, and his first job was at Dunelm, but his heart was never in it. He had other interests outside Dunelm and for a while he was a good amateur boxer but gave that up in his late teens, much to the relief of his mother. He took time out to travel to faraway places – New Zealand, Canada and extensively in Europe – and when he came back he found the company on a roll, with both his parents and his brother fully absorbed in keeping up with store openings and acquisitions. He was a talented boy, who could have developed into a decent retailer if he had put his mind to it, but he could see – which I couldn't – that there was room in the business for only one brother, and that wasn't him. Eventually he went his own way and created a successful property company mainly providing student accommodation. I missed him from the business but had to accept it was the right thing for him.

Will had the benefit of a better education than Jonathan (or me). He was clever and hard-working, and at the age of eleven got into the (fee-paying) Leicester Grammar School, which was 250 yards from the market where he usually joined Jean and me after school. He studied hard in his final year and was offered places by some of the country's best universities, including the London School of Economics. He chose Nottingham to study industrial economics and thoroughly enjoyed it.

But in his final year at Nottingham he developed a health problem so serious that for a time we feared we might lose him. From being an active, strong young man, he suddenly became weak and wan, lost all energy and said he felt awful. Tests showed that he had serious kidney disease, and the doctors told us he would need a transplant. Preferably, it should come from a member of the family with matching blood and tissue. Jean and I both volunteered and the medical people did endless tests on both of us. I am not a hospital-type person and I was dreading the prospect of going under the knife. But to my great relief they decided that Jean, much braver than me, was a more suitable donor and the operation went ahead.

His ambition, even as a young boy, was to own a Porsche and, to pick up his spirits after his kidney operation, I bought him one. But I didn't want Jonathan to think I was favouring Will over him and offered to buy him a car too. Jonathan's big hobby was fishing and the outdoor life, so I offered to buy him a Range Rover. He turned it down. 'No thanks,' he said. 'I'll buy my own car. I don't want to be seen as a Daddy's boy among my mates.'

He ended up buying an old wreck for £200 that made him happier than a brand new Range Rover at many times the price.

Will finished his degree in 1993 but he was still poorly and had to lie down for a couple of hours in the afternoon, and Jean and I were seriously worried if he would ever make a full recovery. I wanted him to join Dunelm where he could set his own pace, and eventually he did although he didn't see a long-term future for himself there. But as his health improved, he began to enjoy himself and eventually asked me could he join full-time. I was only too happy but insisted he smarten himself up. Up to then, he had worn jeans and other casual clothes, which was perfectly reasonable when he was working in the warehouse or driving a van. I was legendarily scruffy myself and often turned up for meetings in a van and my work clothes. That was all right for me, but it would never do for the son of the boss. 'From now on you must wear a suit and tie,' I told him. 'The staff expect it – when you walk into a shop you must set the tone.'

He joined Dunelm at a time of explosive growth, and I needed his help just to keep up with it. After a year or so, I put him in charge of property, and he also did some buying, which he was very good at, as he was at everything – he was a born retailer. I think he got that from me.

Will joined at a time of major change and disruption among our suppliers, most of whom I had dealt with for years. I had always tried to source our merchandise from local manufacturers, but factories all over the West Midlands and the North were closing, unable to compete with cheaper labour overseas. At first the textile industry moved to Portugal then, when that became too expensive, to Turkey and further east: India, Pakistan and today it's mostly in China.

The once mighty British textile industry, once the biggest in the world, consolidated into a single big company, Carrington Viyella, run by an Iranian immigrant called David Alliance, but even that was doing badly. Alliance swallowed most of the big household names, including Nottingham Manufacturing, Viyella, Jaeger, Vantona, Coats Patons, and Tootal. We ended up buying Dorma, whose polyester-cotton sheets had been one of the drivers of Dunelm's growth for years, for a nominal £5m. We've kept the brand alive, and we still sell a lot of sheets under the Dorma name.

Initially, factory closures were good for us, and we were almost swamped with seconds and clearances. But that soon dried up and more and more of our new stock came in from overseas. Will coped well with the changes, which actually widened our range of merchandise and also made them cheaper. But I still mourn the loss of the old mills where I made many friends and golf-partners.

Chapter 16

Takeover Bid

On average, a new Dunelm superstore took three years to recover its costs but once it hit peak performance, it added at least £2m to sales and often a lot more. By 1996 we had ten out-of-town superstores and another five planned, and sales that year leapt by £7m to £22m and profits increased to £3m. We now had more than 300 staff and a fleet of vans and trucks valued at nearly £200,000 – a long way from the bread van I bought for £200 in 1979.

We were becoming a big talking-point in the retail industry, but I hadn't expected to be the target for a takeover bidder until one day I got a call from a County NatWest banker asking to meet me to discuss a potential offer for my company. I had never even talked to a City banker before and was more intrigued than interested, so agreed to meet him and his client, who he introduced as Michael Rosenblatt.

I knew a bit about Rosenblatt, as everyone in the trade did. Originally from Liverpool, he had inherited a small import business from his father, which he expanded into retail and, under the name Rosebys, floated it on the stock market in

1992. The share price, which I followed in the *Financial Times*, had risen rapidly, and he was regularly in the news for making yet another acquisition in a long line of acquisitions. Now, it seemed, we were being lined up as his next target.

From his point of view, his timing was perfect. Until Will arrived, I was really a one-man band, doing everything myself (with Jean's help of course), but I was increasingly conscious that the company was out-growing me and I had to accept, reluctantly at first, that I could not do it on my own. Will, after just two years in the company, was progressing in leaps and bounds but he wasn't yet ready to take over from me.

I was still only forty-eight with plenty of energy and was not contemplating retirement, but, as always, I was fearful about what lay around the next corner and woke up every morning convinced that Dunelm might not survive the day let alone the next recession. Jean and I had already taken out enough money to be comfortable for the rest of our lives, but it was a good time to tidy up the family finances and think about the next stage of our lives.

The thought of selling out for a good price and taking it easy after thirty-three years of seven-day weeks was tempting, and I agreed to enter into discussions, which soon became serious.

I found Rosenblatt an experienced and clever negotiator who in just a few years had used his share price premium to finance a bewildering series of acquisitions, including Fads and Homestyle, well-known high street brands specialising in household textiles. In the two years since his stock market listing, sales had risen from £45m to £69.2m and his shares had quadrupled. The City and the financial press found that impressive but, over the same period, Dunelm's sales had increased from £7.8m to £22m, so we were actually growing faster, which was what attracted him to us in the first place. The acquisition of Dunelm would make him the only serious player in the fast-growing soft furnishings business.

I sent Will out to take a hard look at the Rosebys' shops and his report back was not encouraging. There were, he reported, over 300 of them, mostly small, the kind of high street shops that we were already moving out of. Rosenblatt said he had plans to build his Knightingale brand into a discounter operating out of what he called 'large outlets', which meant about 3,000 sq ft, a tenth the size of our big stores. He talked grandly of Rosebys being a 'value-for-money retailer' aiming to 'match department store quality', but Will could not find much evidence of it. Dunelm was already doing that but in a far more effective way. Will wasn't impressed with the quality and range of their merchandise either: we bought largely from British manufacturers or wholesalers who we knew but more than half his products were imported from low-cost suppliers based in countries like Turkey and Pakistan. One thing was for sure: he was not giving John Lewis any sleepless nights.

We had been negotiating for about a month when Rosenblatt came up with a firm offer: £18 million, which in 1996 seemed like a lot of money to me. But it was in a mixture of shares and cash – mostly shares – which meant I would be swapping my unlisted shares in Dunelm for high-priced Rosebys' paper, making me the biggest shareholder, bigger even than Rosenblatt. Basically, Jean and I would be placing a large part of our wealth in the hands of a smart wheeler-dealer who could do what he liked with it.

To protect the family investment, as a condition of the deal I insisted on appointing a director to the Rosebys' board and proposed Will as deputy managing director. But when I suggested it, Rosenblatt flatly refused. 'We've acquired lots of companies and none of them got a seat on the board,' he said bluntly. 'It's not going to happen.' That caused me to smell a rat and I broke off the negotiations, deciding we were much better off on our own.

Will and I had learned a great deal during the experience and in the following weeks we talked things through. Rosenblatt had managed to float his company, which was not much bigger than ours, on the stock market at a fancy price and since then his shares had risen from 117p to more than £3 in four years. If he could do it, why couldn't we? We had a much better company with a unique retail formula and almost unlimited room for expansion.

This was the time of what one pundit called 'racy' ratings for retail companies and the fast-expanding specialist retailers like Carpetright and DFS Furniture were selling at price-earnings ratios in the high 20s and even 30s. As soon as we saw the back of Mr Rosenblatt, we made up our minds. We would float Dunelm, however long it took. 'You do it,' I said to Will. 'I'll make you managing director and you look after that side of the business.'

From that time on, although we both knew it was years away (in fact it was ten), that was our target, and Will would be the man who drove it. I would stay on as chairman, but the power had passed. From now on, Will was in charge.

We learned another lesson from Mr Rosenblatt. After I turned him down, he went on another takeover spree, and, in 1998, just two years after our talks had ended, Rosebys hit problems and its shares collapsed from a high of 310p to just 60p. But Rosenblatt was a resourceful chap and somehow recovered to go on yet another spending spree, this time acquiring Bensons for Beds, Harveys and Fabric Warehouses, all good names on the high street. Once again, he over-did it, and, in 2008, Rosebys, by then called Homestyle Group, was caught by the recession and high interest rates went into administration.

If we had accepted his offer, I would have lost a large part of the family fortune. It was a salutory lesson never to get into takeover discussions again — and I never did.

Chapter 17

Taking a Step Back

The Rosenblatt takeover and the promotion of Will had profound implications for the future of Dunelm. Will was still only twenty-four and even Jean thought I was taking too much of a risk in making him managing director after less than three years working full-time. But I had seen him through new eyes during the negotiations and was impressed with his maturity and the way he handled Rosenblatt and the City bankers. He seemed totally at home, as if born to it.

Despite Jean's doubts, I never thought it was the right thing to do at that moment in the company's history and time would prove me right. Will and I had different management strengths that, on the whole, complemented each other. At heart, I was a market trader, good at buying and selling and living off my wits; and he was a corporate man, a very good one. There was no way he could have started Dunelm – that was not in his nature. He could not have knocked on factory doors or formed the close friendships that I did with the suppliers who often gave me preference over everyone else. Nor could he have done the wheeling and dealing or taken the risks that I did in the early days, putting the whole business on the line more than once. By the same token I could not have done what he did, putting in place a corporate structure, with a strong board, sophisticated IT and financial systems, and an organisation that would see us all the way through to a stock market listing, our ultimate goal.

Overall, we made a good combination and after some initial nervousness, I let him get on with the job, keeping a wary eye out for signs he had gone too far, too quickly. I kept reminding him that we must not lose the individuality and ethos of the company, and, having grown up in the business, he understood that. But there were occasions when I would find myself having to calm down an irate landlord or manager who felt offended by his sometimes abrupt manner.

Father-to-son transitions are not easy, but this one went remarkably well. I had seen other founders stay on too long, stubbornly refusing to delegate even when their organisations became too complex for one man to manage. Every time I opened my *Financial Times*, there seemed to be another family company in trouble, and I was determined we would not join that unhappy club. By those standards, our transition went relatively smoothly, although there were times when it didn't necessarily feel that way.

People often ask me how I felt about passing executive control of the business to such a young man when I was still in my prime. It didn't happen overnight, of course, and inevitably there was a long period when staff still regarded me as the real boss and came to me for decisions. It took Will some time to establish his authority, but I made it clear to everyone that Will was now in charge and gradually he was accepted as the numero uno.

I was happy – maybe resigned is a better word – to let it happen. My job was basically done, and I only got involved in executive decisions when Will asked me – which was not often. We would work together for the next ten years, during which time I felt entitled to the odd grump and he sometimes ran out of patience. We had our differences of course and the occasional blazing row, mostly over what I considered to be extravagances, spending money on things I wasn't convinced we needed. He was usually right and invariably I gave in, although not always with good grace.

Overall, looking back now, I am rather proud of the manner in which I accepted my role as basically a non-executive. I think Will, who meticulously consulted me on all major decisions, would probably agree with that.

Chapter 18

East Street

In 1997 we bought the old Argos store in East Street in Leicester, our biggest and best deal yet. Argos had moved out and no one wanted the sprawling premises, which included a huge warehouse and an NCP car park that we got for next to nothing. Will found the site and I negotiated the deal, taking advantage of tougher economic times to drive a hard bargain. The East Street building had a huge shop on the ground floor, far too big even for us, and we didn't have enough product to fill it. Will took responsibility for adding new ranges of household textiles, kitchenware and anything else he could get his hands on. It would be our last city centre shop.

At that particular moment in the company's development, East Street was exactly what we needed to take us to the next stage.. It was a big, ugly, rambling building, cut into a hill with one floor at the back and three at the front. There was a tiny office near the rear of the huge warehouse, dark and gloomy, and, at Will's insistence, we turned it into the nearest thing we had yet had to a head office. I moved into what had been the

Argos manager's office and Will took the office next door – I think it was the cash office – which was connected to mine by a hatch through which he could poke his head to speak to me. We shared an assistant, Emma Ashford, who we promoted from the shop floor (she is still with us today).

I have always hated offices and I spent as much time as I decently could away from this one. I went in most mornings at nine o'clock, lit my first cigar of the day, read the *Financial Times*, checked the share prices of my investments and adjourned to the greasy spoon café next door. I spent most of my day out, visiting the stores or suppliers in their own premises.

With Will running the business day-to-day and me contributing my fair share, growth actually accelerated. In one year alone, 1998, we added £10m to sales and £1m to profits (£4m that year), and by the end of the decade, our twentieth year in business, sales topped £70m, and £100m the year after that. Our average growth rate in those five years was nearly 40 per cent a year. And we were still a private company, 100 per cent owned by the Adderley family, who were barely known outside our circle of friends and people we did business with.

Our rapid growth threw up all sorts of issues that I was happy to leave to Will. He kept telling me we needed to install sophisticated technology, from electronic tills in the shops (EPOS, for 'electronic point of sale') to systems to control stock in the warehouses. The Internet was still in its infancy, and online sales were just beginning, but technological change was coming down the road at us with frightening speed, and I knew I would have struggled to deal with it. I had grown up in Woolworths where we dealt basically in cash, which the cashiers physically counted each day, the books being balanced at the end of the week. In the market stalls, almost everything was cash, and Jean on her own, with no professional qualifications, could keep track of it. Dunelm now had more than thirty shops with average sales of £2m a year and we had still barely expanded outside the Midlands and Northwest. The rest of Britain was wide open to us.

Growing the business outside our core area was my job. No matter how far away,

I always insisted on personally inspecting every potential site and negotiating terms with the property agents. I was still the face of the company and never missed the opening of a new store where people expected to see me. Most of the new stores were within driving distance but in 2000 we opened in Dunstable when we were offered a good site, and another, a few years later, in Romford, three hours away by car, just within my driving range.

Weston-super-Mare, which followed a year later, was a slog and Scotland, where we opened our first store in 2001, was too far even for me. But Northern Ireland, where we opened next, was familiar territory and I happily drove myself all the way. I turned up in Belfast in good time for the opening and drove into the car park where the first thing that caught my eye was a large caravan selling tea, coffee, burgers and so on. Ever since Rotherham, I had always liked to have our own café but this, I could see at a glance, was not ours and clearly someone was moonlighting. On further inspection, I noticed an electric cable snaking out from the back of the caravan and running across the tarmac to a hole in the store wall where it was obviously connected to our electricity supply. When I faced the man in the caravan, telling him who I was, he didn't bat an eyelid but said casually he would 'make other arrangements'.

I'd had a long drive so, having my made my point, I asked him for a 'coffee, no sugar', which he made for me.

'That'll be £1,' he said without batting an eye. I couldn't help but laugh and handed him a £1 coin.

Chapter 19

The Sweater Shop

We had never had a real head office until 1995 when we bought a large factory, warehouse and office space in Syston, a small town on the outskirts of Leicester. It had previously been owned by a company called The Sweater Shop, a retail chain which made and sold its own sweaters through its own shops. Founded by a man called Brian de Zille in 1973, it was initially a big success and at its peak it had seventy-eight shops and factories in Leicester, Shepshed, Nottingham and Ayrshire. Then, in 1995, Zille sold the business to his management team for £150m and a few years later the company went bust, put out of business by cheap imports against which it could simply not compete.

Its biggest factory was on Fosse Way, in Syston, which had recently closed with the loss of 1,000 jobs. We bought it from the receiver for £240,000, closed our small office in East Street, which I had always hated, and moved everything to Syston. That gave us the space to build the management team Will had always wanted, many of whom would come from outside the company. Within a year there were more than 100 people in the building, including two ex-Woolworths' managers, Barrie Rees and Gordon Gwynne, who we hired as area managers, a recognition of the speed at which we were expanding into new parts of the country. There were familiar faces too, people I had hired years before and who had worked their way up from the bottom. I was particularly pleased to see Carole Whitley who, alongside Jean, had kept the books almost from the beginning in a pokey little office above the Loughborough store. She now moved into what was to be her first decent office. Carol was a pillar of Dunelm, loved and respected by all. I first met her when she applied for a job at our new store in Loughborough, and I interviewed her, liked her and took her on. She could turn her hand to anything and, as well as keeping the books she also did all the re-ordering of repeat merchandise, which was a big job in its own right. Nothing fazed her.

Carol was one of the team at Fosse Way who had started with me as youngsters. James Rowell was another one. He originally joined the company as a teenager in 1991 when I had just bought Rotherham and within a few years he was a store manager, then area manager and now we made him responsible for Dunelm's entire store opening strategy, one of the most important jobs in the company. He is still there and has been working for the company for thirty-three years. Lisa Allen joined Dunelm as a young girl, moved up to buying and over the years became one of our most successful managers. Ian

Sanders, Colleen White and Mike Carter also started on the shop floor, young people with boundless energy who wanted to get on and we gave them the opportunity. Faye Atkins, who joined as a merchandiser, is another great example of promotion from within – she is now the company's buying director, responsible for hundreds of millions of purchases every year. Most of the new team however came from outside, bringing with them a fresh wave of skills and experience which we could not easily have replicated from within. They were recruited from the big stores groups who were often ahead of us in terms of practice and systems and we were able to learn something from them. But they learned something from us too and the new people were surprised to see how far ahead we were in some vital areas, including store layout, range of merchandise, buying techniques and staff relations.

The newcomers soon settled in and the pace of change, already fast, speeded up, particularly on the IT front where we had lagged for years. When I visited the shops, which I did most weeks, there were automated tills and sophisticated financial and stock controls which were so much better than what we had before. We were late to install EPOS, which was standard in most retail companies from the mid-1990s, and we didn't use barcodes until after most other store groups. Now we were making up for it.

The new systems made everything so much faster and easier. Every part of the business was affected and the staff really appreciated it. Saturday night had always been an anxious time for me as I waited for the weekly figures to tell me how well – or badly – we had done that week. That was easy at the beginning when Jean and I could just add up the cash but the more stores we added, the more difficult it became. In the early days, I used to drive to each store on a Saturday evening after closing time, collect the weekly figures from each manager, go back to the office and add them all up. But when Will took over he would get each manager to call him and fax him the weekly sales figures while I waited anxiously by the phone.

Will would then call me and I knew instantly from the tone of his voice what sort of week we'd had. I'll never forget the evening he gave me the news that we'd done more than £1m that week. We were both jubilant and I must have jumped for joy.

That would have been about 1999. The next year weekly sales topped £2m, and they averaged £3m the year after that. By that stage I was getting the figures on my mobile phone, much faster but less fun than Will's weekly call.

It was a wonderful feeling seeing it all come together, with the new team, new stores, new ranges of merchandise and new IT systems driving sales which rose 12-fold in the 1990s alone.

No other retailer in the country matched that.

Chapter 20

Houses

I have described how Jean and I lived frugally even when the company was doing well. But I always hankered after a decent house, if only to prove to myself I'd made something of my life. Jean and I had begun married life in that little thatched cottage with only an outside lavatory when I was working in Peterborough and we had gradually moved up the property ladder from there.

When I got promoted from Lady Pool Road, my first store as a Woolworths' manager, to Bell Green in Coventry we bought our own house for the first time. It was a four-bedroom detached house in Hinkley, with a through-lounge and a carport on a new estate. I was only twenty-three at the time and very proud of it. It cost me £6,400, and I broke my 'no borrowing' rule by taking out a mortgage. Within a few months I was regretting it. Interest rates went up and so did my monthly payments, causing me sleepless nights. I remember lying in bed thinking what a stupid thing I'd done.

But my salary increased, interest rates fell and house prices rose, so it worked out well. We sold at a good profit and used the proceeds and an even bigger mortgage to buy Dunelm, the house that gave the company its name, in Greenhill Road, Coalville (it was already called that when we bought it, for reasons I never discovered). Then I lost my job at Woolworths and I thought we were in real trouble. My slippers coup bailed me out of that one.

I eventually sold Dunelm and invested the proceeds in one big deal, as I have related, and came within a stone's throw of losing the lot.

After that, as I did well on the Leicester market and the business prospered, we moved steadily upmarket. Someone once said of me that my hobby is moving houses, and it's at least partly true: I usually started off liking a house then got tired of it and found something I liked better. In all, I reckon Jean and I have had twenty-three homes.

As we became better off, people expected us to spend our money on yachts and villas in the South of France but neither of us had the slightest interest in them. I've never been on a yacht in my life, and I've never been into a casino, and I don't want to. But you have to have some visible symbol of success, so I bought Thornhaugh Hall, near Stamford (voted the best village in which to live in Britain in 2013), in Lincolnshire, with 300 acres of land, a lake with its own boat-house and jetty, spacious gardens and a stable courtyard. The house, for which

I paid £10m, looked like something out of Downton Abbey with a grand entrance, a cavernous hallway, a huge drawing room and even a full-size billiard table and billiard room which was bigger than our entire council house in Leeds. I've often wondered what Jean's mother would have said if she'd lived to see it. I remembered her cutting remark to Jean when we told her we were going to rent our first home: 'You've always had grand ideas.'

She was right in one sense: Thornhaugh really wasn't us. Jean and I are not that kind of folk, and we were uncomfortable there. We lived in it for twelve years until we couldn't bear the problems with staff and the upkeep, and we bought a lovely four-bedroom house in the countryside outside Leicester where I intend to spend the rest of my days – until I find something else!

Chapter 21

Stock Market

'For as long as anyone can remember it has been the pride and duty of small businessmen to grow big, to go public and cash in part of their fortune that is wholly locked up in the business.'

Sir Patrick Sergeant, City Editor, Daily Mail

From my earliest days in business, I dreamed of running my own public company with the share price listed every day in the *Financial Times* and our results written up twice a year. It was the ultimate mark of success for any businessman, a public affirmation to the world that you had made it. From the moment we saw off Mr Rosenblatt in 1996 and I made Will managing director, that became our ambition. It was a distant prospect at that stage, but you have to begin somewhere and we began there.

In the first few years we were too busy to give it much attention and it was the early part of the new millennium before we seriously began to focus on it. Will had a school friend, John Sturmey, who was working for UBS, a big Swiss bank with offices in the City of London, and he contacted him, making it clear he was just testing the waters at this stage, trying to get some idea of whether Dunelm was a marketable proposition. He also got in touch with another City merchant bank, Goldman Sachs, just to get a second opinion.

Both came back to say we had a marketable proposition and they would be keen to act for us. However, they also concluded, after a cursory look, that we were not nearly ready and would have a lot to do of work before seriously contemplating a flotation, or IPO (for initial public offering).

Alone in my office one day, I did some rough calculations, trying to work out in my head what the company might be worth if we floated. In 2002, we had revenues of almost £134m and profits after tax had grown 20 per cent that year to nearly £12m. What value would the markets put on that, I wondered? The soft furnishings sector was reckoned to be worth approximately £5 billion a year, spread across a wide range of companies, none of whom specialised in it in the way we did. It was growing at an annual rate well in excess of the economy or general retail sector, which made it more attractive to potential investors. John Lewis was the market leader with 5 per cent, twice our share, but soft furnishings was a minor part of its business, and it was not a direct competitor. In any case, my analysis, gained from walking around the stores (there was a big John Lewis in Leicester), was that their prices were roughly twice ours for the same quality product. For instance, Dunelm sold an Egyptian cotton bath towel for £6.99 while John Lewis stocked an identical one for £16. The same towel, give or take a few square centimetres, was £10.40 in M&S, £13 in Debenhams and £9.99 in Argos. Tesco sold an inferior towel for £7.97. No one could match Dunelm for value for money.

There were lots of out-of-town retail chains by then, including B&Q, Homebase, Comet, Matalan and MFI, but they were all very different to Dunelm. Argos, IKEA, Asda, Debenhams and even Woolworths – still going then – dabbled in the home furnishings sector but none of them was a serious competitor. We were unique.

Running my eye down the list of shares in the Retail section of the *FT* prices page, the first thing I looked at when I opened the paper, I could identify no other company with which we could directly compare ourselves. There were only three companies that were vaguely comparable to Dunelm, although they sold completely different products: Halfords, Topps Tiles and Carpetright. Their average price/earnings ratio, a measure I had picked up from reading the paper closely (share price divided by earnings per share), was fifteen. Carpetright, the most highly rated, was more than twenty, reflecting the high regard in the City for its chairman and founder Phil Harris.

I took a conservative multiple of fifteen times earnings, which, based on 2002 earnings of £12m, gave me a rough value for Dunelm of £180m. But as new stores opened, we were already projecting after-tax profits of £17m for 2023 and £22m for the year after. That, on my very crude calculations, would value us at more than £300m in another few years.

The Adderley family still owned 100 per cent of the equity and I had deliberately not widened the base to include management, as other groups did. Instead of share options, we incentivised the senior managers with generous cash bonuses. A public listing would allow us to grant them options and a stake in the company, which increasingly they were asking for – and would also give Jean and me the opportunity to realise some capital if we wanted to (I didn't but Jean did).

Will eventually chose UBS as our sponsoring bank and John Sturmey introduced him to his boss, Jim Renwick, the head of capital markets who would be responsible for the listing process. Renwick came up to see us and I liked him from the first meeting. He was an impressive man, in his forties, an Australian who did not look – or sound – at all like my image of a typical, stuffy City banker.

I took him out for a game of golf and we had a good heart-to-heart. He told me he had joined UBS in 1990, left for a two-year spell to run a 'boutique' broking house called Bridgewell and, after it was sold, he went back to UBS. He proposed that, if we went ahead with the IPO, we should hire Bridgewell as UBS's co-sponsor – which we eventually did.

Renwick loved the Dunelm business, particularly our sales record, which showed more than twenty years of unbroken growth. He was even more impressed with the fact that growth, far from slowing down, was accelerating. In 2001, sales grew by a third to top £100m, by another 40 per cent in 2002 and, in 2003, when we formally appointed UBS, they again increased by 40 per cent.

But Renwick had other concerns and pointed to a number of issues that we would have to deal with before putting a foot in the City.

First and foremost was our lack of a professional finance director and the sophisticated financial controls that investors would expect. For years, before we moved to Syston, the nearest we had to a finance department was the office above the Loughborough store where the redoubtable Carole Whitley and Jean somehow kept the books with only basic electronic systems to help. Things had improved since then but we were still short of what the City would expect.

Will already had a head-hunter looking for a really good finance director and in the middle of 2004, after interviewing goodness knows how many prospects, he asked me to meet his preferred candidate, David Stead.

I liked him immediately. He was in his mid-forties, ten years older than Will, ex-Oxbridge and had worked at Boots the

Chemist for fourteen years, ending up as finance director. A big reorganisation of the Boots group made his role redundant, and he was now looking for a new challenge. He told me he was bored with working for big companies and welcomed the chance to join a smaller business where he could get in early on an IPO that could make him some decent money through share options.

Towards the end of the interview, I asked him, 'Out of a score of one to ten, how do you feel about joining us?'

'About seven out of ten,' he replied.

I said, 'Well, I feel about seven out of ten about you, so let's give it a go.'

We put together a salary package with the promise of share options and he arrived in September 2004 raring to go. Will and I knew we had hired a real star. Within weeks of his arrival, he was well down the road to putting in place new financial controls and reporting systems. The first big task, he informed the board - which I still chaired - was the integration of a new IT system, which would take several years to complete but would transform just about every aspect of the company, from the tills in the shops to wages, warehouse, stock control, buying – everything. At the centre of it all would be a SAP computer system, which he said was the best available. I sat in on management meetings and tried to keep up with progress, but it was a challenge. I learned more about IT systems in those months than I had in the rest of my life.

David was our most important recruit yet, and joined a team of executives, expert in their individual areas, which Will put together with my approval in each case. For such a young man, Will was remarkably shrewd when it came to hiring the right people, and for the most part I signed them off without hesitation. But I drew the line when he proposed taking on a full-time property director. I saw it as a waste of money and told him he should do the job himself, as he had been doing up to that point, and he stomped out of my office. In the end I grudgingly agreed to meet his proposed candidate, Steve Barton, convinced in advance I would not like him.

Steve turned out to be a very personable young man, in his early thirties, who had worked for Next and Levi Strauss and clearly knew a lot about the retail property market. The more we talked the more I warmed to him, and at the end of our interview I was as enthusiastic about him as Will was. He turned out to be an outstanding success, accelerating the speed at which we opened new stores and upgrading the older ones. I'm not sure how we would have managed without him, particularly in the period leading up to the IPO in 2006 when we were opening new stores at a rate of nearly one a month. It took a bit of time but eventually we put in place a superb team of executives with a broad range of high street experience: Tim Slade, like David Stead, came from Boots to take responsibility for store operations; Mark Guerin, responsible for central operations, had worked at Homebase. We had others who came from Superdrug and M&S, so the new team covered the spectrum of British retailing at that time.

There was so much happening on the corporate front that it was very easy to take our eyes off the trading side of the business, which at the end of the day was what we were about. We had a big store opening programme planned, which would not fully kick into profits for several years, and somehow we had to keep up the momentum before the IPO. We planned to open ten stores a year between 2002 and 2005, and by 2006, the probable date of the IPO, we reckoned we would have sixty-five stores. We were still operating mostly in our core territory, the Midlands and Northwest, and even after our big opening programme, we would still have only two stores in the Northeast, four in London and none along the southern coast (and one in Belfast of course). That left plenty of room for expansion, which would please the City.

Soon after he arrived, David Stead recruited Ian McMillan, a fifty-year-old seasoned techie who had been round the houses a bit, having worked for M&S, Superdrug and, most recently, Kingfisher. He arrived in late-2004 and hit the ground running, taking charge of the IT team already working under David's direction. His early report to the board was sobering: even if the team worked around the clock, he reckoned it would take up to three years to bring the new system fully on stream, which would take us to 2007, well past the 2006 IPO deadline we were aiming for. To my surprise, the advisers took that in their stride – no IT system, they said cheerily, ever came in on time or on budget and so long as we could show we were well down the road, it would not be a problem.

They later covered themselves by adding a note to the prospectus, which, under the heading 'Potential Risks Facing the Company', recorded that Dunelm had replaced its original IT systems 'which were not considered capable of supporting the business in the short to medium term'. That was partly my doing – I had resisted, until it was almost too late, Will's determination to bring the systems up to date.

Another initiative of Will's, which proved important to the future prosperity of the company, was to enter the relatively new world of online retailing. Dunelm's first web store was based in the Radcliffe warehouse, run by Sara Way, a bright young sales assistant whose potential Will spotted at an early stage. She was promoted to take charge of building the website, where she did a fantastic job. It was up and running by 2005, just before the planned IPO. In retrospect, that was a big moment for the company and another milestone that was totally down to Will. Initially, online sales were a tiny proportion of the total, but they grew and grew until in 2023 they accounted for 36 per cent of sales of more than a billion. I don't think online will ever completely replace the bricks and mortar of stores – we need both. Customers love to come into our stores just to browse, and the company encourages it. Often, they will see an item that they later buy online.

Bridgewell, as co-sponsors of the IPO, prepared a detailed report aimed at attracting potential investors, and its analysts trawled through every detail of the company. They loved what they called our 'unique format', by which they meant that we were the only homewares retailer trading in out-of-town shopping centres, offering a 'range dominant' proposition – typically 16,000 to 18,000 lines in a single superstore. They were also greatly impressed with our own-brand merchandise, but what struck them most was the value for money we offered while keeping our margins high and growing the business.

We were well down the IPO road when the City advisers raised the issue of my future role. I had blithely assumed that I would take the company all the way to the stock market as chairman, but the advisers didn't think that was a good idea. Dunelm, they advised, would need a strong board of directors, including at least two well-known 'independent' names from the City – one of whom should replace me as non-executive chairman. The City rules and regulations, put in place after some of the big public scandals in the 1980s, disapproved strongly of a father–son combination running a public company. 'It contravenes the Code,' one of the lawyers told us solemnly. 'And breaks every rule put in place in the past twenty years. One or the other of you is going to have to step aside.'

I had been studying the rules too but I was the founder and thought I could get away with it. This was my company. I had built it, I was the controlling shareholder, and I didn't want to step aside so close to my life-long dream of taking it all the way to the stock market. That dream, which had kept me going in some of the darker times, was now dead. But I was still in charge of the board with the right to have a major say in choosing my own successor.

First, we had to appoint an independent non-executive director, and we were fortunate to find Marion Sears, who David Stead knew and highly recommended. Importantly for us, she was very familiar with the City where she had worked for several of the big merchant banks, including JPMorgan and Robert Fleming. She was also, as I was to discover, an exceptionally nice person who lifted the tone of our little board from the moment she arrived. She proved a godsend, providing invaluable advice and wisdom on how to navigate our way through the complex rules of corporate governance.

Finding a new chairman was a trickier task but again we were lucky. The head-hunters came up with a shortlist of candidates and Will and I interviewed them. One stood out, head and shoulders above the others: Geoff Cooper, a qualified accountant and former finance director of the Gateway (later Somerfield) supermarket group. We offered him the job and he proved a great choice. Any residual resentment at losing the chairmanship vanished soon after he arrived, and I don't think we ever exchanged a cross word.

Geoff and Marion immediately went to work to help David Stead ,who was working around the clock to prepare the prospectus. Someone gave me an early draft which clearly set out my new status and put me firmly in my place. Under the heading 'Directors, Senior Management' it said 'Bill has gradually handed over leadership responsibility to his son, Will, but remains involved in strategic matters at Board level. He continues to promote core values of customer focus and "Simply Value for Money" throughout the group. Bill intends to remain as Non-Executive Director until the age of 60.'

That gave me just two years to go.

To my surprise, I quite enjoyed the IPO process. I'd never had much contact with the City before and had long held the view that most City people, instead of wearing pinstripe suits and bowler hats, should have been dressed in balaclavas and carrying shotguns, because they were crooks, preying off people like me who worked our guts out to build a business while they were lunching in their posh club. But we were either lucky in our choice of bankers or I had greatly misjudged the City. Jim Renwick had first opened my eyes to the possibility that City people could behave like normal human beings and I soon discovered he was not an exception. There wasn't a pinstripe in sight when I visited the UBS office in a modern building near Liverpool Street Station, and no mahogany panelling or large partners' desks. I attended several meetings in the offices of the lawyers, Allen & Overy, one of the top City firms, and it was much the same. They seemed perfectly normal people.

Some of the meetings were enormous, up to thirty people, at least half of them women, mostly in their late twenties or thirties. There were two sets of lawyers, one to advise us, the other to advise UBS and the brokers, Bridgewell, the two sponsors of the issue; the auditors, KPMG, advised both sides, presumably for two sets of fees. Dress was casual, with no ties and rolled up shirt sleeves, lunch was a Pret a Manger sandwich at the board table and no one drank anything stronger than water or the odd Coca-Cola. I was disappointed by that – I was half-hoping for lunch at the Savoy Grill with a champagne aperitif.

Every person around that table was charging exorbitant fees, which at the end of the day Dunelm would have to pay and, as a 50 per cent shareholder, half of that would be mine. Looking around at these earnest, young and likeable people, each expert in their own particular disciplines, I couldn't help thinking back to my first day as a Woolworths' manager of the Ladypool store when I sacked the window cleaner because I was personally paying 10 per cent of his cost. That probably saved me about £2. In this room, that was not even one second's fees. But they knew what they were doing, and, in the end, I came to admire them.

The advisers did endless calculations and comparisons to arrive at a value for Dunelm, which, for all their sophistication, was not that much different from the one I had done on the back of an envelope several years earlier. They finally came up with the recommendation that we should offer 60m shares (out of 200m) to the public at a price of £1.70, valuing the company at £340m. No new shares would be issued and all the shares on offer would come from Jean who would take out more than £100m in cash and keep a 5 per cent stake worth another £30m.

At the end of the long meeting to settle the issue price, one of the advisers turned to me and asked, 'Are you happy with £1.70? Have you any problem with that?'

'Look,' I replied, 'I'm a market trader, I'm a shopkeeper. When I go to Majorca, I don't get on the plane and ask the pilot to see his pilot's licence. I assume he knows what he's doing. Why are you asking me? I know bugger-all about that.

I paid you guys because you're good and you're pros. I'll take your word for it. If you say £1.70, then it's £1.70.' I looked around at the sea of baffled faces. Clearly they had never had a client like this. 'And if anyone has a problem with that five years from now,' I added for emphasis, 'I'll give them their £1.70 back. I promise you.'

There was a silence before someone remarked, 'You're not greedy, are you?'

In their experience, people listed their companies on the stock market to get rich and would argue over every penny. When someone asked what I was going to do with the money, I replied, 'I'm not doing anything with it. I watch television at home, and I have the odd drink at the pub. I don't go in casinos and I don't sit on yachts, so I'm not doing anything with it.'

As soon as the issue was announced, we were besieged by journalists, particularly the local papers in Leicester and Leeds who saw us as big news. They wanted to interview me of course, but I had never given an interview in my life and was not going to start now. Will handled it all, with his usual calmness and skill and we got a favourable press.

I think every newspaper in the country wrote about us, mostly along the lines of 'Rags to Riches' (a witty variation was 'Swags to Riches') and the 'husband-and-wife team who built a retail giant from a single stall in Leicester market', which was fine with me. The more serious papers, which were what mattered, liked the proposition and the *Daily Telegraph* recommended the shares as a 'buy' at £1.70.

Some of the press reports revealed aspects of our customers we were never aware of. One lady from Kent contacted the regional manager to tell him that she visited the Dunelm store in Canterbury every single day of the week. She didn't buy much, she said, she just liked being there. A columnist in *The Times* admitted she did much the same thing in the store in Birmingham. 'I used to drive to see my mother,' she wrote, 'with the added bonus that I could pop into the Dunelm in the city and fill the car, stopping the orgy of shopping only when it became impossible to see out the back window.'

We never knew until then that we had such a group of loyal shoppers.

The issue in October 2006 was a big success and the shares got off to a flying start, hitting 190p in their first week of trading. And, with some bumps along the way caused by setbacks in the markets, they went on going up.

Chapter 22

Raid on M&S

One of my biggest regrets in later life was that I never made a big takeover bid when I had the chance. I kept identifying companies I itched to get my hands on, convinced I could have turned them around in no time. There were always stores in trouble and I know I could have rescued them. I had been hanging around shops since I was a boy of eight, making myself a nuisance or doing odd jobs for a few bob, and I knew a bit about the trade. I still go into shops today and I find it hard to believe they're still in business.

I watched with envy as Philip Green bought the Arcadia Group with a wonderful array of brands, including Topshop, Dorothy Perkins, Debenhams, Principles, Racing Green and Evans, and then destroy it. All the great department store chains of my youth, Debenhams, House of Fraser and Sears, were taken over and broken up. I could have done that and have often wondered why I didn't.

My biggest handicap as a businessman was that, unlike Philip Green, I had grown up in a culture where if you couldn't afford a bike, then you couldn't have it. Later, when I was earning a bit of money at Woolworths, I bought a small second-hand car. No HP. By the time I discovered the benefits of borrowing, I was a multi-millionaire and didn't need it. I take a lot of pride in the fact that I took Dunelm from a stall in the Leicester market to the London stock market without borrowing a penny.

But I know I could have done better, and Dunelm could have grown even faster if I'd accepted some of the money the banks were queuing up to offer me. Whatever my differences were with Woolworths, they taught me how to run a store, skills that I could have used to manage a much bigger business. I should have gone to the banks, borrowed a billion pounds and taken over one of the big retailing groups that were in trouble. I would have made a better shot at it than Philip Green.

I would have had a lot of fun and made a lot more money. But I didn't and let the moment pass.

But if I couldn't buy a whole group, I could at least buy their shares. After I left Dunelm, I contented myself for a bit with playing the market, buying shares I thought were cheap, selling when they became over-priced. I lost some but, on the whole, I made money – a lot of money. After the financial crash in 2008–9, which was followed by the steepest recession for forty years, retail shares fell to absurdly low levels. Even Dunelm was not immune. Between 2008 and 2010, the low point for the economy, the company increased sales by more than £100m to half a billion, but its shares suffered along with everyone else's. They briefly hit 200p and then in early 2009 they sank right back to 90p, less than half the peak. On paper that had lost me £170m but I wasn't bothered – Jean had more than £100m in the bank and I had put something aside too for a rainy day.

I have always been a punter in shares, taking large positions in a few companies rather than smaller stakes spread across the board. I like to bet against the herd and recessions have been good times for me. I enjoy pitting my wits against the most sophisticated analysts in the City, and while more conventional investors were losing money hand over fist in the recession, I was making it.

M&S continually caught my eye as the shares sank from a high of 700p in 2007 to under 200p (they're not much more today). In my years at Woolworths, we envied M&S, which took over our position as the biggest and best-loved stores company on the high street (maybe in British history). It seemed incredible to me that it could go so wrong in such a short time, and I was convinced that, whatever its fall from favour, there was value there.

I began buying when the shares were at rock bottom and when they recovered to 250p, I bought some more – and I went on buying. I did it quietly, through several brokers, and no one noticed. M&S was going through a particularly rough time, sales of clothing were down, and it was taking a hammering from the competition – and from City investors who had turned against it. It was the perfect time to mount a bid, but the company's problems were daunting, and no one was brave enough to take it on. Philip Green had a go at it in 2004 and never fully recovered his reputation after Stuart Rose, a man I admired, saw him off.

Later, Green got into big trouble over the BHS pension fund and his whole high street empire came crashing down around his ears. Green's flagship company, British Home Stores, once the only real rival to Marks & Spencer, was eventually sold for just £1. He left the City in disgrace with demands he be deprived of his knighthood (as far as I know, he's still got it).

I had no time for Green as a man or as a retailer. I only met him once and that was enough for me. I was reasonably well known by then and featured in the *Sunday Times Rich List* – probably above him – and at a black-tie dinner at the Dorchester a number of big names in the retail trade came over to my table to say hello.

I spotted Green in the lobby afterwards and went up to him, just to shake his hand, one retailer to another, and introduced myself. 'Mr Green, I'm Bill Adderley. I'm pleased to meet you.' And I held out my hand to shake his.

'I've never heard of you,' he said rudely, dropping my hand as if I had the plague. He turned his back and walked off, wiping his hand on his jacket. Not a nice man.

When I became seriously interested in M&S, it was run by a Dutchman called Marc Bolland who was well into a three-year plan that involved investing more than £2 billion on upgrading the stores, many of which hadn't had a penny spent on them for goodness knows how many years. But despite all his efforts, sales of clothing went on falling, which wasn't a surprise to me – the stores were like morgues, and, on my regular visits, I was sometimes the only person in the men's department. The women's wasn't much better. But there was value there and I went on buying until I had spent more than £200m, a fair chunk of my net worth. It wasn't long before the share price turned, partly as a result of my purchases, and I found myself sitting quietly on a profit that no one knew about other than me. I didn't even tell Jean.

The company took some time to wake up to my interest but when eventually it did I had a call from Bolland's office to say he was coming up to Leicester and could we have lunch in the local M&S store. I never turn down a free lunch and happily went along, interested to hear what he had to say. Bolland was all charm and insisted on giving me a guided tour of the store, trying to illustrate the difference he was making to the group's merchandise, after which we had lunch in the staff canteen. We talked politely about the retail business, and he asked me what I thought, and it was some time before we got to the subject he wanted to raise: What was my interest in M&S? Why was I buying?

'Because the shares are cheap,' I replied truthfully. 'I see it as a good investment opportunity. That's all.'

He clearly didn't believe me, but he was careful not to push me. He knew the Adderley family controlled a two billion pound company and if I wanted to I could make myself a real nuisance.

A few days later the company invited me down to London, gave me a tour of their huge head office followed by a detailed financial presentation, clearly prepared for their big institutional shareholders and largely wasted on me. I went on hunch and experience, not on detailed research available to anyone. Then we had lunch in the very grand boardroom, attended by half a dozen executives who were very guarded in my presence. After that I went down every eight weeks or so, just for a catch-up and a free lunch.

I continued buying shares, driving up the share price, until I passed the 3 per cent mark, which was a mistake. The City rules required M&S to put out an announcement revealing this, and suddenly I was on the financial pages of every newspaper.

Bill Adderley unmasked as Marks & Spencer's biggest private shareholder

Guardian, October 31, 2013

'Bill Adderley, the billionaire founder of the homeware chain Dunelm, has secretly built a near £250m stake in Marks & Spencer, it has emerged,' reported the *Guardian*. 'The entrepreneur acquired the shares during the past 18 months, a period in which the M&S share price has risen by almost 40%.'

It created something of a sensation in the market and the financial press followed it up for days. One of the retail analysts was quoted as saying: 'He's brave to take such a big punt on an M&S recovery.' But what did the analysts know? None of them had ever run a shop in his life. I had built a whole retail chain.

I wasn't used to being in the news, but I was secretly pleased when one of the papers commented that my presence as a shareholder was a 'credibility boost' for M&S. Dunelm was a star performer and my reputation as a retailer had never stood higher, even though technically I had retired.

I refused to talk to the press, but I got a financial PR man to brief several of the journalists on an off-the-record basis, pointing out that if I was really going to make a bid, 'this would be an extraordinarily clumsy way of going about it'.

I had a high regard for Mr Bolland who I thought was a good CEO and got M&S moving in the right direction. The markets thought so too, and the share price began to recognise it. He left before he could complete the job.

That was also the time for me to depart. I sold as quietly as I had bought, with not a single headline or comment in the press.

I made a handsome profit and moved on. My one regret was missing my regular lunches in the M&S boardroom with the directors. I had greatly enjoyed them, the first – and only – time I moved in that kind of company with people as interested to hear my views as I was to hear theirs.

Alas, once I sold my shares, I was never invited again.

Postscript

9 July 2024

From its foundation in 1980 right up to the pandemic in 2020, Dunelm grew both its sales and profits every year, thirty-two years of uninterrupted growth, which must be some kind of a record. From total revenues of £44,000 in our first year, which Jean and I considered a big success, sales topped the £1m mark in 1985, £100m in 2011, £1 billion in 2018 and in 2023 they were £1.64 billion. Or if you look at it another way, sales were £880 a week in our first year, which was an awful lot of curtains sold on our 12 sq ft stall in Leicester market. Sales are more than £30m a week now, sold in 180 beautifully laid-out shops. Profits have kept pace, topping £200m in 2023, which is £4m a week.

I can still remember saying to Jean, just a few days after we started trading on the Leicester stall, 'I think we're on to something here. One day this could be very big.' At the time we barely knew where the next meal was coming from, but I had seen enough to realise I had strayed on to something special, that I was good at it and it had considerable potential. My imagination stopped short of a £2 billion company, but I certainly saw a much bigger business than just our little stall.

It started off as just Jean and me, but as soon as Will and Jonathan were old enough to help, they worked alongside us. Will went on to become managing director at the age of twenty-four and gradually took over from me to take the company – with my help and support – all the way to a stock market listing and beyond. Growth has been phenomenal since then, first under Will and the superb management team he put together, and later, after he too stepped down because of ill-health, under new management who carried on where the Adderley family left off. The shares hit a peak of £14 in 2022. During that eighteen-year period, Dunelm has paid out £1 billion in dividends, equivalent to £10 a share.

Today Dunelm is the largest soft furnishings retailer in the country. When I opened our first superstore in Rotherham, the market was dominated by John Lewis, and we were not even a speck on the chart. Dunelm's market share was 2 per cent when we floated in 2006 with sixty-five stores. In 2013, we passed John Lewis to become the Number One. Market share has gone on growing every year since, while John Lewis, which we all held in thrall, has tumbled back down the league tables, much of its magic gone.

These figures disguise the enormous amount of effort, skill and risk, first under me, then under Will, it took to get Dunelm to where it is today. It has changed of course as it has evolved and online sales have boomed, but it is still recognisably the same business I put together thirty years ago. I moved on from the market stall to open my first shop in 1984, which led on naturally to the store in Rotherham in 1990, the first large store in Britain dedicated solely to homeware. No one else was doing what we did, and no one is doing it today, at least not with anything like the same passion or focus. Rotherham was the model for everything that followed, a 30,000 sq ft out-of-town store, offering a wide range of soft furnishings at 'value for money', a principle I set from the beginning and that was the real secret to Dunelm's success.

Today's Dunelm stores are marvels to me, all that I dreamed of and much better. They are bright, with better displays and a much wider and deeper range of merchandise and yet they are still recognisably based on the Rotherham model. The look and feel have not changed recognisably since those early days.

Another Dunelm attribute I can take some credit for is its reputation as a good employer. That has been absolutely central to the company's expansion. When we were smaller, I knew most of the staff by their first names and maybe the names of their children as well. Later on, as we grew bigger and that was no longer possible, I spent a lot of time going around the shops, talking to people and listening to their problems. I encouraged everyone to call me 'Bill' and it wasn't just for show – I preferred to be on first-name terms which always broke the ice. I like people, and I was genuinely interested and concerned about their problems, and they saw that and responded to me, always greeting me with a smile.

Today there are 11,000 people who work for the company, 250 of whom have been there for more than twenty-five years, some of them hired by me when they were only teenagers. I have always believed in giving young people a chance, just as Woolworths gave me a chance as a Saturday boy. Few ever let me down and some of them really excelled. They became friends as well as colleagues and when someone retires after thirty years of service, it is me who they want to get their award from. I usually make a speech recalling the days when the company was in its infancy and we'd be out in the van together chucking stuff through the door.

We made a preferential offer of shares to staff when the company listed and those who took advantage of it – not enough – are better off today than they ever dreamed of. I remember taking on a sixteen-year-old joiner's assistant who turned up for his interview with a big black eye – he'd been in a fight with his boss and lost both the fight and his job. He was a super lad who is now on the junior board of directors where he looks after all returns and has saved the company many millions of pounds. He's one of several who have made themselves millionaires by working from the ground floor up in Dunelm.

Will would be the first to acknowledge that he inherited a company that was already established and in very good shape.

POSTSCRIPT

But in turn I am the first to acknowledge my good fortune in having a son with the retail and management skills to take the business to the next stage. We have also been fortunate in the chairmen – three of them so far – who succeeded me: Geoff Cooper, my immediate successor, was an outstanding success and Andy Harrison, former chairman of the RAC, Whitbread and half a dozen other companies, who succeeded him, was even more so – a very impressive man. Now we have Alison Brittain, former CEO of Whitbread and chair of the Premier League, Dunelm's first woman chair and another success. We've had some real heavyweights to take the company on and, successful as it is today, its greatest days still lie ahead.

Jean and have also been very fortunate in the next generation of Adderleys who have brightened our older years. In 2001, Will, after a long courtship, married his long-time girlfriend, Nadine Rose, who went to the same school as he had. She is five years younger than him, so they didn't meet until much later by which stage he had recovered from his kidney problem and was rapidly moving up the ladder at Dunelm.

We hadn't even known about Nadine until one evening she called at the house to collect him. In those days he finished work just in time to dash home for a quick shower and change before going out at eight. On this occasion he had left it late and was still in the shower when the doorbell rang. Jean answered to find this very pretty girl asking for Will – and that's how Nadine Rose came into our lives.

A few days later Will introduced her to us properly, and we both loved her from the start. She is a Leicester girl, one of four daughters of well-known chiropractors in the town, Colin Rose and his French wife Genevieve, who had their own clinic on London Road.

She and Will couldn't have seen much of each other in the first few years of their courtship. Will was putting in gruelling hours, seven days a week, and she was away at university in Bournemouth, then worked for a year for a jewellery shop in the town after which she went travelling for six months. It was 2001, seven years after they began courting, before they actually got married; Will was twenty-nine and Nadine was twenty-four.

Their little girl, Ava, was born in 2003 and brought back memories of our own little daughter Theresa when she was a tiny baby. I make no apologies for calling her my favourite granddaughter – until recently she was the only one. She was followed closely by their two lovely boys, Freddie and Cedric (Fred and Ced).

Jonathan also had two great boys, George and Charlie, by his former partner Jenny, who has done a great job with them. The relationship broke up a few years ago and Jonathan now has a new partner, Monica, and a new little baby Eve who is already challenging Ava as my co-favourite granddaughter.

POSTSCRIPT

It's interesting to me now how Leicester, wholly by chance, has been at the centre of all our lives for nearly fifty years. It was basically an accident, or fate, whatever you want to call it, that caused us to settle there in the first place. I had been moved so often by Woolworths that, when I was appointed manager of the Coalville store, a few miles outside Leicester, Jean and I decided the time had come to put down some roots. The boys were at the local school, and we couldn't keep moving them, so I took a deep breath, got a mortgage for more than I could afford and bought Dunelm in Greenhill Road, Coalville, the house that gave its name to a national stores chain today. I left Woolworths a few years later and the rest is history. I rented a stall in the Leicester market for fifteen years, basically because it was close to Coalville; I opened my first shop in the town centre; and we had our first headquarters just outside. Dunelm now has a very grand office and large warehouses at Syston, five miles outside Leicester centre, on the site of the old Sweater Shop.

When he was awarded an honorary degree by the University of Leicester in 2024 Will remarked, 'Leicester is where I have lived since I was five years old. It is where I have worked my whole career, it is where I got married, and it's where our three children were born.'

Will and Nadine were just settling into their family life when Will's kidney problem re-occurred. It got so bad that he had to step down from his position as CEO of Dunelm, still in his thirties, although he stayed on as deputy chairman. He needed another kidney transplant, and this time his brother Jonathan very generously donated one of his. Will briefly returned to the CEO spot a few years later when his replacement didn't measure up, but stepped down again although he remains as involved as ever. He is still the biggest shareholder. Since I left Dunelm, I have enjoyed my golf, travelled a bit, mostly to Spain or South Africa, and watched a lot of football. I do a bit of fishing still and I collect Irish art. I still go to Donegal every summer, as I did when I was a young boy, driving myself all the way there and back.

I still don't have a house in the South of France, no yacht and no great mansion but I toyed with the idea of buying a vineyard in the Cape Winelands, which is a beautiful place, or a golf course in Spain, but, in the end, I pulled back – they're too much hassle and I want a quiet life. I bought a house in London but sold it again (to the head of Google, said to be worth $40 billion, which puts me in my place). I am no good at charities and have little interest in politics, which is why I suppose I have remained just plain 'Bill Adderley' when much less successful businessmen have been knighted or sent to the House of Lords.

Jean is much better at charities than I am and has always given away more than enough for both of us, even in the early days when we couldn't afford it. The big donor in our family is Will and I take my hat off to him for his commitment to so many causes, putting almost as much energy into them as he did into running Dunelm. In 2007, after Dunelm floated and he had a bit of money, he founded the Stoneygate Trust, which has supported over 500 projects in Leicester and Rutland, where he now lives, and his donations include one for £10m for the new Stoneygate Centre in Leicester University. The university awarded him an honorary doctorate, his second.

He spreads his charitable donations widely but concentrates on kidney disease research to which he has given away goodness knows how many millions. Even after all these years of research, there is no cure for kidney disease but there are drugs that can slow it down and prolong life expectancy. One day, who knows? I hope he lives long enough to see a real breakthrough.

One of the proudest days of my life was when the Queen awarded Will a knighthood for his services to charity and he and Nadine became Sir Will and Lady Adderley. We all went up to Windsor Castle for the ceremony, performed by Princess Anne, and I kept thinking how far we had come in three generations from that little cottage in Clonmany and the council house in Leeds.

It's been a long but wonderful journey, from Donegal, to Leeds, to market stall in Leicester and finally to a £2 billion company quoted on the stock market. I wouldn't have traded it for anything.

Appendix

Stamford School Lecture

I never made many speeches in my life but on the rare occasions I did, I thoroughly enjoyed it, and I like to think my audience did too. Ever since I was a small boy, I had no stage fright, and one of my teachers always said I could have had a career on the stage if I'd had the opportunity. At Dunelm, I made speeches at leaving parties or other events, and staff told me it wasn't the same when they got someone else. I never made any notes, but I knew what I wanted to say, and it came out without hesitation or repetition. I had no trouble getting and holding people's attention.

    The speech – more a talk – of which I am most proud was the one I gave to a class of teenagers in the local school, and I shall try to recreate it here, or as much of it as I can, from memory. For a time, as I have described, we lived in Thornhaugh Hall, near Stamford, the grandest house we ever owned. One of our neighbours was a delightful man called Mike Pring, a civil servant who had a connection with the local Stamford school. I was becoming fairly well known by then and Mike asked me if I would give a talk to the sixth formers, a mixed group of sixteen-year-olds, who were studying business, and maybe inspire a few of them to follow in my footsteps.

I would do anything for Mike and readily agreed. The other speakers, he told me, would include his son Nicholas, the co-founder of Urban Pubs & Bars, a successful chain of pubs and eateries based in London.

The first speaker was a farmer who droned on about the benefits of growing potatoes in Lincolnshire, which caused half the class to fidget and the other half to fall asleep. I half-listened and thought to myself, 'This is not going to be a hard act to follow.'

The farmer talked from behind the teacher's desk at the front of the classroom, but I decided to do it differently. I strode into the classroom from the back, walked past the students, all of whom had their backs to me, and plonked myself down on the desk, facing the room. Everyone other than me seemed nervous and when one of the teachers brought me a cup of tea, the whole class room could hear the rattle of the cup in the saucer.

'I don't know what I'm doing here,' I eventually started. 'I know nothing about business.' I paused, letting that sink in. 'But I know if I changed my money into £10 notes, they would not fit into this room.' That got their attention, and I could see the heads pick up. 'I am also the cleverest person I've ever met!' I pointed at one of the mystified faces. 'And so are you!' I swung round to include the whole class, jabbing my finger towards them. 'And you! And you!'

'So don't ever let teachers put you down,' I said. 'Being good at a subject is great but it's not for everyone. Wayne Rooney and David Beckham were told by their teachers they would never be any good, but if Beckham rang that teacher today, he would walk on broken glass to get him around for dinner.'

I then took them through my basic life story, starting with the council house in Leeds, my family, four in a bed and my wasted school years. 'My problem at school was that I just didn't see the point of it,' I said. Most of my classmates ended up working in a warehouse or on the factory floor. I still feel they should have been teaching them the practical things of life, preparing them for the world they were actually going to have to live in. None of us ever became scientists. Good manners, which should be learned at school, beats an A-Level any day.'

The point I really wanted to get across was that academia was not for everyone, a view that didn't go down well with the teachers.

I then went on into my fifteen years at Woolworths where I started as a fifteen-year-old Saturday boy in Leeds sweeping the floors and worked my way up to be manager, a big job with a lot of prestige in those days. 'And then I fell out with Woolworths and I had no job and Christmas was coming on. I had a mortgage, a wife, two children and just £800 in the bank. I was desperate, really desperate. I would have done anything to provide for my family. I had no pride – and I don't do shame. But, as things turned out, leaving Woolworths, which was all I'd known up to then, was the best thing that ever happened to me.'

I told them the story of buying the bread van for £200 and spending the rest of my precious money on a load of reject slippers that I bought for 50p each. I told the class, 'I took a vanload of them down to the market in Leicester the next morning, but I couldn't get a stall even though I was first in the queue. That was the lowest point of my life.. I thought I'd lost everything: I couldn't get a job, I had no money, I had gambled everything on a deal that hadn't come off and I couldn't meet the next mortgage payment. But you have to keep going. The next day I drove down again, bribed the man to give me a stall – it cost me £10 – and the slippers sold like hot cakes at 99p a pair. In three weeks, I sold out, making a profit of £8,000.

'But I still didn't know what I was going to do next,' I went on. 'Then one day I got a load of ready-made Marks & Spencer curtains and shoppers on the market queued up to buy them. And that was the beginning of Dunelm, which is today worth two billion pounds. And the Adderley family, although we've sold some shares, still owns nearly half of it.'

I certainly had their attention by then and they looked at me with a new respect. But I had not yet come to the point I wanted to make.

'You can do it too – you can all do it. What's the worst that can happen to you? What if you were to go home today and tell your parents you're leaving school and you and your boyfriend or girlfriend are going to open a burger caravan on the A47? Your Dad would bollock you and probably call me, asking me what kind of ideas am I putting into young people's heads. He would say, he wants you to be a doctor, an accountant, a lawyer, maybe even a soldier. But if you really want to do it, no one can stop you.'

I wanted to get them thinking a bit differently, maybe spark an entrepreneurial spirit in even one of them.

'Starting your own business is like being in love,' I went on. 'John Lennon didn't have to ask his mother if he could start a band. He just went ahead and did it. If you take a girl home and tell your dad you love her and you're going to marry her, he will probably disapprove. After she's gone, he may tell you, don't ever bring that girl home again.

'So what do you do? Do you dump her? If you do that, you didn't love her in the first place. So when you start something, don't listen to anyone. Starting a business has got to be a passion.'

They told me afterwards that I spoke for an hour and a half, and at the end people wanted me to go on. But I had been invited to lunch with the headmistress so I had to stop. Over lunch, one of the teachers asked me if I would have a word with her husband. 'He lost his job two years ago, but he's very

STAMFORD SCHOOL LECTURE

proud and won't take another without the same title and the same car. What can I do?'

I wasn't sure how I could help her with that.

I was on again after lunch and this time it was standing room only.

I had more fun that day at Stamford School than I'd had for years. I loved watching the faces of those teenagers change from boredom to rapt attention and even admiration. I was even more thrilled a few days later when I got a letter from a group of them saying they'd had a collection and wanted to meet me again to take me to lunch.

Those reading this book may think that's no big deal, but I have just four O-Levels, grew up in a council house and started in business on a market stall. Gaining and holding their attention was important to me, more important even than doing another deal. Alas, the teachers didn't see it that way. I'd had a go at the school system and was never invited again.

But I like to think that somewhere out there is at least one budding businessman or woman who learned something that day and was inspired enough to do something about it. I hope so.

Acknowledgements

There are so many people I want to thank for their incredible help and support in turning Dunelm from a market stall into a successful stock market company. While I can't name everyone, and I may have forgotten some, there are a few people who truly deserve special mention:

    David Baldwin
    Julie Bell
    Rick Bullbrook
    Paul Fitzpatrick
    Barbara Inchley
    Richard McIver
    John Phipps
    Jack Rogers
    Kevin Rutherford
    Dinesh Shah
    Chris Taylor
    Simon Taylor
    Tony Taylor

Thank you all for everything you've done for Dunelm and the Adderley family. I couldn't have achieved this without you!

                            Bill Adderley, Stamford, May 2025

Index

Abbreviations are used as follows:
Bill Adderley (BA); Jean Adderley (JA); Will Adderley (WA).

acting 40
Adderley, Bill
  PERSONALITY: ambitions 54; attitude to wealth 162–164, 179, 196; bargaining skills 87–88; business dress 143–144; charm 122; informality 137; self sufficiency 38
  CHILDHOOD: church attendance 37; education 40–43, 199–200; elastic band factory mischief 33–35; family poverty 27–28, 33, 35–36; holidays 11–12, 15–18; moneymaking schemes 35–36; parents 31–33; stands up to bullying 38
  PERSONAL LIFE: first girlfriend 51–52; driving lessons 56–58; first date with Jean 65–67; engagement and marriage 70–72; children 73; homes 2, 162–164; partnership with JA 89–90; father and sons in business 141–144, 151–153, 192–193; friendship with Keith McIver 133–135; with Mike Winch 104; grandchildren 193–194; hobbies and interests 31, 41–42, 55–57, 104, 133–138; psychic powers 94–95; religious beliefs 18–19, 72; retirement 196; connections with Leicester 195
  BUSINESS SKILLS and VALUES: borrowing 181–182; buying British 134, 144–145, 148; the City 176–177; computers 129; display 130; education 42–43, 199–200; grudges 101–103; management skills 61–62, 151–153; office work 155; public companies 165; respect 62; special offers 131; speech-making 198; staff 78, 137–138, 191–192; starting a business 151–152; stock market investments 182–183; takeover bids 181–182; trusts experts 178–179; up front payment 89, 101, 116, 118, 181–182; value for money 89, 118, 191;

205

working with sons 151–153;
young people 75–76, 192,
202–203

CAREER: WOOLWORTHS:
Saturday job 44–46, 49–51;
trainee manager 52–53;
promotions and moves 55–56,
59–63, 68; skills learnt 51,
61–62, 63–64; disenchantment
with 74–79; demotion
and resignation 1, 80–82;
unemployment 1–2

CAREER:MARKET TRADER:
home deliveries 2–3; starts
selling 3–9; early days 84–88;
buys new car 86; partnership
with JA 89–90; business model
84–88, 92–93; buying stock
99–106; successful trading
114–116; mistakes learnt from
96–99; diversifying range 118;
Saturday sales 110–114, 132;
gives up stall 132–133

CAREER: DUNELM: name
107–109, 195; first shops
119–122, 124–125; expansion
plans 125–126; acquisition of
Rotherham store 127–131;
tablecloth deal 133–135; buys
Dorma 144–145; steps back
from managing director role
151–153; takeover offer for
146–150; proposes stock market
floatation 149–150; buys East
Street 154–155; growing the
business 156–157; preparations
for IPO 165–180; share issue
177–180; staff relations 159–
160, 191–192, 192; cashing up
160–161; dislike of IT 155–156,
173; turnover 116; steps aside
174–176

CAREER: LATER: Marks &
Spencer 183–188; retirement
196

Adderley, Bridget (née Gill, mother
of BA)
childhood 11, 15, 18
meets JA 68
motherhood 24–25, 27–29, 34–
35
personality 32–33

Adderley, Jean (née Thornton)
personality and interests 66–67,
68, 138, 196
education and early employment
66–67, 72
courtship and marriage 65–72
children 73, 90–91, 142–143
supports BA's resignation 81
market trading 3–5, 8, 116–118
Dunelm 124, 178
accountancy skills 90–91
wins miners' sweep 117–118

Adderley, John Joseph (father of BA)
personality 28–31
wartime service 21–26
employment 26–27, 39
driving lessons 58
meets JA 68

Adderley, John Joseph (grandfather of
BA) 21

Adderley, Johnnie (brother of BA)
28–29

Adderley, Jonathan (son of BA) 73,
112–114, 141–143, 194, 195–196

Adderley, Kathleen (sister of BA)
24–25, 28–31

INDEX

Adderley, Peter (brother of BA) 43
Adderley, Philip (brother of BA) 34
Adderley, Theresa (daughter of BA) 73
Adderley, Will (son of BA)
  birth 73
  education and employment 112–114, 127–129, 141–143
  career 143–144, 149–150, 151–153, 154–156, 168–171, 190
  charitable giving 196–197
  honours 195, 197
  health 142–143, 195–196
  personal life 193–194
Aldridge, Arthur 42
Allen & Overy 177
Allen, Lisa 159
Alliance, David 144
Angela's Ashes (McCourt, Frank) 27
Argos 154
Asda 74
Ashford, Emma 155
Atkins, Faye 160

B&Q hardware chain 76
Bargain Brands 77
Barton, Steve 171
Beck, Charlie 54–55, 79
bedspreads 97–98
Belfast 156–157
Berni Inns 65–67
Birmingham Woolworths 62–64
Bolland, Marc 185–186, 187
boxing 41
Brayshaw, Tony 84–85, 87, 115
Bridgewell 168–169, 174
Briggate Woolworths 48–52, 54–55
Briggs, Mrs (teacher) 40–41

Brittain, Alison 193
Bubb, Nick 187
bullying, childhood 38
buyers at Woolworths 54–55, 78–80
buying for Leicester market 3–4, 85, 87, 92, 101

cafés 128–129, 157
cakes 45, 49–51, 59, 97
Candlelight Homewares 103–104, 106
car boot sales 96–97
Carpetright 167
Carrington Viyella 144
Carter, Mike 160
chairmen of Dunelm 175–176, 192–193
charitable giving 196–197
childcare 90–91
Childs, Keith 3–4, 8
Christmases, childhood 33, 35–36
City, the 176–177
Clonmany, Donegal 11–12
Coalville 100, 108–109, 117, 121–122
Cohen, Jack 123–124
comptometers 66–67
computerised till systems 129
confetti 113–114
Cooper, Geoff 175–176, 193
Corpus Christi Secondary school 41–42
cost savings at Woolworths 63–64
Cotton, John 101–103, 106
cricket test matches 94
crockery 59–61
curtains 84–85, 100–101, 115–116, 140

207

de Valera, Éamon 25–26
directors, board of 174–176
Dodds, John 81–82
Dorma 100–101, 105, 106, 107–109, 144–145
driving lessons 57–58
dry-cleaning clothing deal 98–99
Dunelm
  name 107–109, 195
  business values 89
  shops: first shops 119–122; out-of-town stores 139–140, 146; Rotherham store 127–131, 191; store openings 171, 172
  online retailing 173–174
  IT 155–156, 160–161, 170–171, 172–173
  head office 154–155, 158–161
  recession 182–183
  management: management team 158–160, 192–193; financial directors 169–171; WA as managing director 151–153; successor to BA 174–176
  employees 78, 137–138, 140, 156–157, 191–192
  Roseby takeover bid 146–150
  preparations for IPO 165–171
  shares 168, 177–180, 183, 192
  turnover and sales 116, 119, 124, 125, 146, 148, 155, 160–161, 166, 167–168, 189
  uniqueness 166–167, 174, 191
  value for money 89, 140, 167, 174, 176

economic recession, 1970s 76–77
elastic band factory escapade 33–35
engagement rings 70–71

factory sales, Saturday 111–114
families and business 151–153
farming at Clonmany 12–13, 15–18
favoured buyer status 101
financial controls 169–171
financial integrity 89
fishing 17
Fogarty 105–106, 114
football 41

Gill, Kate, (grandmother of BA) 12–13, 15
Gill, Willie (grandfather of BA) 12–14, 15, 16, 18
golf 133–138, 196
Graham, Mark 112
Graham, Matthew 112
great grandparents of BA 14
Green, Philip 181–182, 184
Gregson, Yvonne 92–93
Guerin, Mark 172
Gwynne, Gordon 159

Harris, Phil 126–127, 139, 167
Harris Queensway 126–127, 139
Harrison, Andy 193
Head, Mr (Fogarty) 105–106
head office, Dunelm 154–155, 158–161
home deliveries 2–3, 55
Hull 44

Iceland 77
Ingleton, Jonathan 112
IPO, preparations for 165–180

John Cotton 101–103
John Lewis 126, 140, 148, 166–167, 190

INDEX

kidney disease 142–143, 195–196, 197
Kingfisher 82–83
knighthood, WA's 197
Knightingale brand 148

Ladypool Road Woolworths 62–64
Leeds 26–29, 39, 48–52, 54–55, 65, 122–123
Leicester
  Adderley family and 195, 197
  Dunelm 120–121, 154–155
  market 5–8, 110–111, 132–133
literacy 13, 14
Loughborough 111

magazine sales 96–97
management skills at Woolworths 59–61
market traders 5–8, 86, 122–123, 132–133
Marks & Spencer
  BA and 85–87, 92, 183–188
  history 122–123
  Woolworths and 53, 74
Marks, Michael 122–123
Marshall, Bob 49–50
McIver, Keith 133–135
McMillan, Ian 172–173
mining 117–118

newspaper reports 179–180, 186–187
Nott, Derek 101, 105, 107

online retailing 173–174
out-of-town stores 127, 128–131, 139–140, 190–191
overages 79–80

palm readings 94–95
Parish, Gerry 126
pea picking 66
Peat Marwick (KPMG) 66, 72
pillows, Fogarty fundraising 114
potcheen 24–25
poverty 12, 14–15, 33
price crowding 79
Pring, Mike 198–199
property management 171
psychic powers 94–95
public companies 165, 174–175

Queensway Discount Warehouses 126

Ravensbourne Society 136
recession 182–183
Redcar 61, 65
Rees, Barry 159
reference for good service 92–93
religious observance 18, 37–38, 72
Renwick, Jim 168–169, 176
reward system at Woolworths 62–63
Rex Cinema, Coalville 121–122
Riverdale Curtains 84–85, 115
Robinson, Ken 41
Rose, Nadine 193–194
Rosebys 146–150
Rosenblatt, Michael 146–150
Rotherham Dunelm store 128–131, 139, 157, 190–191
Rowell, Jim 159

Sanders, Ian 159–160
Sears, Marion 175
Second World War 22–26
seconds 3–5, 85, 92, 100–101
shares, Dunelm 177–179, 183, 190, 192

shares, Roseby 149
Shaw, John 135–136
shoes 3–5, 97
shopper loyalty 180
shrinkage 79–80
Skegness 81–82
Sketchley 98–99
Slade, Tim 171–172
slippers 3–5
soft furnishings 92, 166–167
  see also curtains
special offers 131, 140
speeches 198–203
Spencer, Thomas 123
sport 41–42
St Philip's Catholic Junior Primary 40–41
staff culture at Dunelm 137–138, 140
Stamford School lecture 21–22, 198–203
Stead, David 169–171, 172
stock market floatations 149–150
Stoneygate Trust 197
store openings 156–157, 171, 172
Sturmey, John 166, 168
Sweater Shop, The 158
Syston 158–159

tablecloth deal 133–135
takeover bids 181–182
televisions 33
Tesco 123–124
textile industry 92, 144–145
Thornhaugh Hall 163–164
Thornton, Mrs (mother of JA) 69–71, 86, 164
Three-Day Week 76
trainee managers 49–50, 52–53, 59–61

UBS 166, 168–169, 176–177
unemployment 1–2

value for money 83, 89, 140, 167, 174, 176
VAT 90–91

warehouse, first Dunelm 107–109
Way, Sara 173
White, Colleen 160
Whitley, Carol 159
Winch, Mike 103–105
window cleaners 64, 177
'Wolfie' (market trader) 86
Woolco superstores 75
Woolworths
  history 47–49
  heyday 46–47
  buyers 54–55, 78–80
  decline and takeover 74–80, 82–83
  managers 49–50, 52–54, 59–61, 62–63, 77–80
  price crowding 79–80
  stores 48–52, 54–55, 62–64
  see also Adderley, Bill

Yates, Albert 41

Zemansky 70
Zille, Brian de 158